Invasion of the Holy Spirit

Intimacy with the Holy Spirit

Volume 1

Pastors Eric & Janet Melwani

Copyright 2017

Biblical scriptures taken from KJV

SPECIAL THANKS

We want to thank and honor our Heavenly Father, Lord Jesus Christ and the Holy Spirit.

We want to honor Apostle Guillermo and Prophetess Ana Maldonado.

We want to thank and honor Pastors Pablo and Alis Vega from King Jesus Ministries, Orlando.

We want to thank and honor our parents and our families.

We want to thank and honor Apostle Mary Smith, Dr. Fernando Gonzalez, Apostle Judy Karim, Bishop Arnold Gajramsingh and Dr. Reuben Egolf for their endorsements.

We want to thank all the members, spiritual family and friends of Church of Many Waters for your love, prayers and support.

We also want to honor Pastor Maxine Sweeting, Prophet Kevin Thomas, Apostle Ludwig and Prophetess Amanda Hodge, Dr. Shashi and Asavari Jatiani, Apostle Lionel and Margaret Etwaru.

TABLE OF CONTENTS

Foreword	Pastor Pablo Vega
Chapter 1	Ruach Ha-Kodesh
Chapter 2	Mind of the Holy Spirit
Chapter 3	Holy Spirit our Comforter
Chapter 4	Ruach Elohim
Chapter 5	Demonstrations of the Anointing
Chapter 6	Ruach Elohim Chayim
Chapter 7	The Holy Spirit's Purpose for Us
Chapter 8	Holy Spirit is a Parent to Us
Chapter 9	Eternal Spirit
Chapter 10	Fellowship with the Holy Spirit
Chapter 11	Manifestations of the Holy Spirit
Chapter 12	Blessings of the Holy Spirit
Chapter 13	Holy Ghost in the life of Jesus
Chapter 14	Names of the Holy Spirit

Chapter 15   Prayers

Chapter 16   Testimonies

FOREWORD

This book on the Holy Spirit is a book inspired by God for these times and this generation. This book is what the Church of God needs to achieve the abundant life that Christ promised after ascending to Heaven. The Holy Spirit is not only the third Person of the Trinity, but is in us, the most important Person for us now.

Jesus said that it was necessary for Him to go so that the promise of the Holy Spirit would come. I am proud of my son, Pastor Eric and Prophet Janet because they have allowed the Holy Spirit to inspire them to translate into a book what is necessary for the Church of God to know, so that we may represent and live according to the promises of the Father.

Pastor Pablo Vega

King Jesus International Ministry, Orlando

ENDORSEMENTS

Drs. Eric and Janet Melwani have taken the subject of the Holy Spirit and made Him as the Bible intended; a living being who desires relationship, to impart revelation, and to empower us to higher dimensions of glory. His workmanship is no better demonstrated than when He works the person of Jesus in us and through us. The conviction of sin, caretaking of the conscience, and breathing of power in and through His people is evidence of a God who loves us beyond our comprehension. The Holy Spirit's contact with mankind is proof of the active grace of God demonstrated every day.

This book will leave you appreciating the best friend on earth we will ever have – The Holy Spirit! Thank You Drs. Eric and Janet Melwani for knowing this friend so well. We as readers are forever indebted.

Dr. Reuben Egolf
United States Global Leadership Council

This book on the Holy Spirit is a much needed resource for those who are desiring to know more about the Holy Spirit. God has used Prophet Eric Melwani mightily and profoundly to have completed such revelation on the topic of the Holy Spirit.

Prophet Eric Melwani is a true man of God. He has true and sharp prophetic insights. I highly recommend this book to everyone.

Apostle Mary Smith

Faith Victorious Lighthouse Ministry

St. Marteen

This publication of the Melwanis on the Holy Spirit exemplifies very fundamental and yet profound scriptural Truths which each believer should become aware of in order to grow into a relationship with the Holy Spirit. It was an honour to read the manuscript and offer helpful suggestions.

I recommend this information to all Bible Study groups and other students of the Bible. I pray that you will find this experience with the Holy Spirit quite fulfilling as you seek to know Him and to impart His power to many.

BISHOP DR. ARNOLD GAJRAMSINGH

I CARE CHRISTIAN CENTRE

TRINIDAD & TOBAGO.

Prophet Eric and Pastor Janet Melwani have been afforded the amazing opportunity and distinct privilege to receive the revelation of the understanding on how the operation of the Holy Spirit progresses, advances, and proceeds in all areas of our lives.

The tactical procedures and implementation models set before you in this book are divinely inspired, so make no mistake about it that you will be lead to a deeper reality of who the Holy Spirit is in your life. You will learn how to identify with the very essence of His existence, thus allowing you to have the greatest of appreciation and reverence for the Holy Spirit as you learn not to take Him for granted.

This Holy Spirit filled manifesto gives you a direct impartation of almost a euphoric experience with the HOLY GHOST leaving you with an in-depth look at your life and what God wants to do with you, through you, and for you.

We bless and honor Prophet Eric and Pastor Janet Melwani.

AMB. Fernando M. Gonzalez Ph.D.

Ambassador at Large to the "Principality & Sovereign Nation of Monte de Agrella"

President of the United States Global Leadership Council (USGLC)

In this book, Prophet Eric Melwani identifies a fundamental need within the Body of Christ today and that is a need for a Holy Ghost invasion. The early Church was born in a unique manifestation of the power of God by the outpouring of the Holy Spirit upon the early disciples. It became a powerful, dynamic organism that was able to convert the entire known world without books or technology in less than two hundred years.

Through in depth research, divine revelation and his own personal experience with the presence and power of the Holy Spirit, the author seeks to educate believers and emphasize the vital need for the fullness of the Holy Spirit. If, we are to impact this generation.

Apostle Dr. Judy Karim

Greater Love Christian Centre

Trinidad & Tobago

Introduction

Ruach Ha-Kodesh Invasion

Acts 2:2-4 says, "And suddenly there came a sound from heaven as of a rushing mighty wind, and it filled all the house where they were sitting. And there appeared unto them cloven tongues like as of fire, and it sat upon each of them. And they were all filled with the Holy Ghost, and began to speak with other tongues, as the Spirit gave them utterance."

On the day of Pentecost, as one hundred and twenty disciples were gathered in the upper room in unity, waiting and expecting the Promise of the Heavenly Father to come. Suddenly, there was a powerful invasion, as the **Ruach Ha-Kodesh** in Hebrew for the **Holy Spirit**, came from heaven to earth in the force of a rushing, mighty wind full of power and might. Jesus had to ascend to heaven, after His resurrection, in order for Him to send the Holy Spirit to earth to be with us and in us.

He knew that we cannot lead our spiritual lives without the help of the Holy Spirit. It says in **John 16:7-8," Nevertheless I tell you the truth; It is expedient for you that I go away: for if I go not away, the Comforter will not come unto you; but if I depart, I will send him unto you. And when he is come, he will reprove the world of sin, and of righteousness, and of judgement:"**

This was a heavenly takeover, a revolution and an invasion of the Spirit of Glory invading the planet earth. That day, the supernatural church of Christ was born and the Holy Spirit came to live within human vessels and make His abode within us. He came to live within those who will obey Him and submit to His presence.

His invasion and coming was so sudden, heavenly, violent, and forceful that it made a sound. That sound was the sound of the movement of the Spirit of God as He rushed through the air waves, currents and laws of the earth realm. He came in power proclaiming His invasion with a new sound to establish the Kingdom of God on earth.

Whenever the Holy Spirit is about to launch a new work, Jesus first sends His word. That released word creates a new sound and that new sound creates waves of glory and power. His mighty power brings into manifestation the unseen from the supernatural dimension into the natural dimension. Thus, He came on the day of Pentecost to launch a new supernatural church being birthed after the works of Jesus Christ. Thus, a supernatural church and a global movement of the Holy Spirit was born as a result of the completed work of the Cross and the shed blood of Jesus Christ.

Ruach Ha-Kodesh came like a rushing mighty wind declaring that He cannot be stopped, hindered, blocked or contained. Like a storm, He came to announce the birth of the supernatural church that will impact all corners of the earth and build a Kingdom of His power and presence.

The invasion of the **Ruach Ha-Kodesh** brought the fire of God from the Heavenly Father and into their inner beings. He filled them with His glory and fire. It was so dramatic, powerful and tangible that their tongues were on fire and burned after they were filled and empowered by the Spirit of God. Thus, His burning fire rested within them, overflowed through them and was released through their tongues as they were filled with the invading power of the Holy Spirit. That day, ordinary men were transformed into supernatural vessels of fire, full of boldness and courage.

The result of the invasion of **Ruach Ha-Kodesh** was an overflow of power from within them. They were given the promised Gift from the Heavenly Father who came forth in His glory and majesty. The third Person of the Trinity released a new sound. The new sound created a new movement. The movement of **Ruach Ha-Kodesh** created a cry from the heart of Abba Father to draw all men into an intimacy with Him through the workings of the Holy Spirit.

Thus, they spoke in new tongues as the Spirit of God gave them utterances. They spoke in several languages they had never learned. The impact of the Holy Spirit's invasion was so great that many of different nationalities, including Jews came where the disciples had gathered. Every man heard them speak in their own language declaring the works of God. This was a supernatural event.

The Spirit of God came to create a "suddenly" movement of glory on earth and manifest His power. Thus, He had a plan and a purpose to draw all men to Jesus Christ and restore a supernatural, intimate relationship with them. He wants to see souls saved and come into the saving knowledge of Jesus Christ. He is the One who reveals Jesus Christ to us and makes Jesus intimately real to us.

Also, every move of God comes like a mighty rushing wind on the wings of **"suddenlies"** to create a Holy Ghost movement with a new sound. It cannot be contained, placed in a box or limited. It is totally supernatural and totally the workings of God. It comes to shake everything that can be shaken, changed and transformed.

The Person of **Ruach Ha-Kodesh** is still here on earth and His mission is to set each one of us from within on fire for Jesus. He is here to walk with us, abide in us, and commune with us and to have an intimate relationship with us. He is the Source of power given to us as a Gift by the Heavenly Father. He is also the source of all victory. Our lives will never be the same again as we come into an intimate relationship with the Person of the Holy Spirit.

Today, let **Ruach Ha-Kodesh** invade your life with His power and presence. Allow Him to manifest in you the "suddenlies" of God. As you draw closer to Him and build an intimate relationship with the Holy Spirit, your life will never be the same again. I welcome you into a new walk and journey with the Person of the Holy Spirit.

Chapter 1

Ruach Ha-Kodesh

Ruach Ha-Kodesh or the Holy Spirit is God. He is also the third Person of the Trinity. He is one with the Father and with His Son Jesus Christ. God is a Trinity, but yet One.

Holy Spirit is a Person. Many people do not treat Him as a Person. They don't even relate to Him as a Person. Many think that He is a fire, wind, dove or a pillar of fire. But, the Holy Spirit is a Person who has His own distinct nature, personality, character, emotions, will and purpose.

Many people do not build a personal relationship with Him. They talk about the Holy Spirit without having an intimate relationship with Him as a Person. Thus, they lack power, His presence and don't understand His wondrous workings.

Ruach Ha-Kodesh is mentioned in Genesis and is involved in the work of the creation. **Genesis 1:2 says, "And the earth was without form, and void; and darkness was upon the face of the deep. And**

the Spirit of God moved upon the face of the waters." We see the Holy Spirit involved in the creation process. Here we see the ability of the Holy Spirit to move and hover upon the face of the waters. As He moved upon the face of the waters, He released His creative powers in the natural. He actively moved, and through His movements the universes were formed during the creation process. Thus, the Person of the Holy Spirit manifested the will of the Heavenly Father through the spoken command of Jesus Christ.

Holy Spirit invaded the waters and created an environment for His presence. As He moved, He also was the breath of God released from the mouth of the Heavenly Father. Expelled breath that is released also carries the dynamics of force and power within it. Thus, as the Father breathed out, life manifested in the creation through the expelled power of the Holy Spirit. Also, the word "Spirit" is translated as "wind" or "breath" in the Old Testament.

Thus, the Godhead willed the creation in existence. Jesus Christ, Son of God, spoke into existence the will of God. Finally, the Person of the Holy Spirit manifested and executed the will of God through creating everything in this creation.

In the book of **John 1:1-3 it says, "In the beginning was the Word, and the Word was with God, and the Word was God. The same was in the beginning with God. All things were made by Him; and without him was not any thing made that was made."** Jesus is the Word and all things were made by Him. Thus, the Trinity being One, created this entire universe by working together in perfect unity, oneness and absolute divine order.

Also, in **Psalms 33:6 it says, "By the word of the Lord were the heavens made; and all the host of them by the breath of his mouth."** Let me give you a revelation. Out of the mouth of the Heavenly Father was released the Word. That Word is Jesus Christ, who commanded the will of the Heavenly Father and created the heavens.

Then, out of the same mouth of the Heavenly Father also was released His breath. His Breath refers to the Person of the Holy Spirit who brought everything into manifestation. Thus, God created the heavens and all the hosts of heaven by **His Word and Breath**.

Further, in **Psalms 33:7 it says, "He gathereth the waters of the sea together as an heap: he layeth up the depth in storehouses."** As we read earlier, Spirit of God moved upon the face of the waters, we see that He was working on His creation and to bring forth life to inhabit the earth. Thus, Holy Spirit was actively creating because He loves to create beautiful things, breathe life in it and call it good.

Holy Spirit loves designs, patterns and is an Eternal Artist. We see His matchless beauty designing and creating in **Job 26:13, "By his spirit he hath garnished the heavens; his hand hath formed the crooked serpant."** Thus, He designed the heavens with His majesty.

In Genesis 1:26, "And God said, Let us make man in our image, after our likeness; and let them have dominion over the fish of the sea, and over the fowl of the air, and over the cattle, and over all the earth, and over every creeping thing that creepeth upon the earth. So God created man in his own image, in the image of God created he

him; male and female created he them."** What is interesting is that God said let **"us"** make man in our image. The word **"us"** refers to the Trinity. It clearly speaks about **God the Father, God the Son and God the Holy Spirit.**

The second interesting point to be noted in this scripture is that it says **"Let us make"** man in **"our"** image. These pleural terms again refers to the works of God, the Trinity**. "Us"** is not a singular term but rather a plural term. Thus, man was made by God, the Trinity. God made man in the image of God as a triune part being**. He was created as a spirit with a soul living in a body.**

The first thing that God did after creating man in His own image was that **He blessed them and commanded them to be fruitful, multiply, replenish the earth and subdue it. He also gave them dominion, power and authority**. The blessings of God activated the power of the Holy Spirit in their lives to be fruitful, bring multiplication, replenishment, ability to subdue and take dominion over everything. They needed the Holy Spirit to help them walk in the commands of God and in the blessings of the Creator.

We read in **Genesis 2:18, "And the Lord God said, It is not good that the man should be alone; I will make him an help meet for him."** God knew that Adam would be lonely so He created a companion or a wife for Him. God being relationship minded gave Adam a suitable help-meet whom he can talk to and have an intimate relationship with. This also is true for God. He created Adam and Eve so that God could commune with them and have a relationship with His first created family. Holy Spirit loves families and He was the Creator of the first family.

Genesis 2:19 says, "And out of the ground the Lord God formed every beast of the field, and every fowl of the air; and brought them unto Adam to see what he would call them: and whatsoever Adam called every living creature, that was the name thereof." It was the Holy Spirit who formed every beast, every fowl and creature but yet He allowed Adam to decide what names he would give them. After Adam gave them a name, it was so and honored by the Lord God.

Chapter 2

Mind of the Holy Spirit

One of the greatest revelations you need to receive about the Holy Spirit is that He is a Person. He has a mind of His own and He has the ability to think, feel emotions, make decisions and exercise His will. He is the All-Knowing God and He governs the kingdom of God and also is involved in the affairs of the earth.

God the Holy Spirit also intercedes for us with groanings that cannot be uttered, according to the will of God. He prays for us, strengthens us and helps us in our weaknesses and areas we are deficient in. It says in **Romans 8:26-27," Likewise the Spirit also helpeth our infirmities: for we know not what we should pray for as we ought: but the Spirit itself maketh intercession for us with groanings which cannot be uttered. And he that searcheth the hearts knoweth what is the mind of the Spirit, because he maketh intercession for the saints according to the will of God."** This scripture also proves that the Holy

Spirit has a mind and He searches the hearts of men and does everything in accordance to the will of Jehovah God.

Holy Spirit has His own will and does everything in accordance to His sovereign will. He even gives us spiritual gifts according to His will. We see that in **1 Corinthians 12:11," But all these worketh that one and the selfsame Spirit, dividing to every man severally as he will."** The will of the Holy Spirit is the will of the Heavenly Father and His Son Jesus Christ. We also see in **Numbers 11:25," And the Lord came down in a cloud, and spake unto him, and took of the spirit that was upon him, and gave it unto the seventy elders: and it came to pass, that, when the spirit rested upon them, they prophesied, and did not cease."**

The Holy Spirit also has a voice. He has the ability to speak and communicate. It says in **Psalms 29:3-4, "The voice of the Lord is upon the waters: the God of glory thundereth: the Lord is upon many waters. The voice of the Lord is powerful; the voice of the Lord is full of majesty."** We also see in Revelations 14:13 that the Holy Spirit speaks and communicates. It says in **Revelation 14:13, "**

And I heard a voice from heaven saying unto me, Write, Blessed are the dead which die in the lord from henceforth: Yea, saith the Spirit, that they may rest from their labours; and their works do follow them."

The Holy Spirit chooses and decides when He wants to come and wants He wants to depart. He has the ability to come upon someone, anoint them and use them for God's glory as they yield to Him. But, He can also depart from a person who does not honor Him and refuses to obey His voice. We see in **1 Samuel 16:14 says, "But the Spirit of the Lord departed from Saul, and an evil spirit from the Lord troubled him."** We also see in **1 Samuel 16:13, "Then Samuel took the horn of oil, and anointed him in the midst of his brethren: and the Spirit of the Lord came upon David from that day forward. So Samuel rose up, and went to Ramah."**

You can only have an intimate relationship with the Holy Spirit by first knowing Him as a Person. Intimacy with Him will cause you to know the mind of the Holy Spirit and His ways. It will help you to understand His divine emotions, patterns, feelings, desires, ways, thoughts and expectations. Only a relationship can produce intimacy. If you don't know Him, then you won't know nor understand His ways, standards, divine emotions, thoughts and His movements. Thus, in order to know the mind of God, we must have an intimate relationship with the Holy Spirit.

Exodus 35:21 says," And they came, every one whose heart stirred him up, and every one whom his spirit made willing, and they brought the Lord's offering to the work of the tabernacle of the congregation, and for all his service, and for the holy garments."

Holy Spirit also has the ability to stir the hearts of others, to touch their will and help them to make the correct decisions. As a Person, He has the divine ability to bring inner transformation and influence others in the ways of truth. Thus, as a Person of the Godhead, He can affect inward changes in others. He also has the power to anoint us for service and to speak the word of God. It says in **2 Samuel 23:2, "The Spirit of the Lord spake by me, and his word was in my tongue."**

Holy Spirit also has emotions. He can be emotional because He is very sensitive. He easily responds to love, worship, praises, faith and obedience. Yet, He hates sin and has zero tolerance for sin. Thus, He can get upset, vexed, quenched and grieved. This is why Paul tells us in **1 Thessalonians 5:19, "Quench not the Spirit."** He also says in **Ephesians 4:30," And grieve not the holy Spirit of God, whereby ye are sealed unto the day of redemption."** He can easily withdraw Himself where He is not welcomed, not received and is ignored. He is the God of Honor and dishonor hurts Him.

When a leader refuses to flow with the Holy Spirit, refuses to obey His leadership and voice then He leaves that place, that service and that ministry. He cannot stay in a place where His leadership is not honored and men have their own ideas, plans and agendas apart from the will of God. **Romans 8:5 says," For they that are after the flesh do mind the things of the flesh; but they that are after the Spirit the things of the Spirit."**

Also, the religious spirit today has replaced the genuine move of God with men's traditions, ideology and fleshly programs. Many people get intimidated when the Holy Spirit starts moving powerfully and they shut it down because they can't control the workings of the Holy Spirit. Thus, the Holy Spirit gets quenched and they insult the move of the Holy Spirit.

Isaiah 63:10 says, "But they rebelled, and vexed His holy Spirit: therefore he was turned to be their enemy, and he fought against them."

Some of the observations we see in the above scripture is that the Holy Spirit is referred as a "He." It signifies that He is a Person. The scripture does not refer to Him as an "It."

The second observation is that the rebellion of the people caused the Holy Spirit to react. He was vexed and upset at their rebellion.

The third observation is that He fought against them. This is because He has the ability to respond and oppose, fight back and respond in the way He chooses and desires.

The fourth observation is that He can also get vexed. He has the ability to feel pain, grief, emotions and He also suffers when people reject

Jesus Christ. Oh, that hurts His heart when people say no to God and walk in their stubborn ways.

Ephesians 4:30 says, "And grieve not the holy Spirit of God, whereby ye are sealed unto the day of redemption."

What grieves Him are found in:

1) **Corrupt Communication-** Ephesians 4:29, " Let no corrupt communication proceed out of your mouth, but that which is good to the use of edifying, that it may minister grace unto the hearers."
2) **Sin-** Ephesians 4:31, "Let all bitterness, and wrath, and anger, and clamour, and evil speaking, be put away from you, with all malice:"
3) **Lack of sensitivity-** Hebrew 3:13 says," But exhort one another daily, while it is called To day; lest any one you be hardened through the deceitfulness of sin."
4) **Disobedience-** Ephesians 2:2 says, "Wherein in time past ye walked according to the course of this world, according to the prince of the power of the air, the

spirit that now worketh in the children of disobedience."
5) **Lack of Honor- John 8:49 says," Jesus answered, I have not a devil; but I honour my Father, and ye do dishonor me."**

Spirit of God is very sensitive. **He hates corrupt communication, lack of sensitivity, sin, disobedience, dishonor and evil ways.** The Holy Spirit is easily grieved when we choose to sin and disrespect Him by acting contrary to His word and ways.

Corrupt communication includes gossip, lying, hateful talk, idle words, evil communication and anything that promotes sin and rebellion. He doesn't stay where sin is glorified and righteousness is rejected. Thus, these sinful ways grieves Him especially when it comes from someone who proclaims to be a child of God.

He is also hurt by behaviors that promotes hypocrisy. He is the God of Truth and He loves integrity, truth and righteousness. When people proclaim the name of Christ from their mouths, and yet are comfortable with sin and compromise. Then, it hurts the Holy Spirit. Many leaders act one way from the pulpit and yet live contrary to God's word in their private lives. Thus, many people are fooled because they see the gifts of God in operation through a vessel publicly without seeing their true character and ungodly ways in their personal lives. **Romans 11:29 says," For the gifts and calling of God are without repentance."**

Holy Spirit is also grieved by those who rebel against Him. Especially those who claim to have a relationship with God and yet choose to disregard His voice by doing whatever they want to do. Some people purposely execute what is in their hearts, despite knowing what God requires of them and is the will of God.

When people become stiff necked and refuse to listen to the Holy Spirit through a hardened heart it grieves the Holy Spirit. **Isaiah 30:1 says, "Woe to the rebellious children, saith the Lord, that take counsel, but not of me; and that cover with a covering, but not of my spirit, that they may sin to sin:"**

Chapter 3

Holy Spirit our Comforter

John 14:26 says, " But the Comforter, which is the Holy Ghost, whom the Father will send in my name, he shall teach you all things, and bring all things to your remembrance, whatsoever I have said unto you."

The Holy Spirit is also called the Comforter who has been sent by the Heavenly Father in the name of Jesus Christ. He has been sent to comfort us, make the presence of Jesus very real to us and manifest the presence of God within us. He comforts us with His reassuring presence that we are not alone. He tells us that He is with us and within us. He comforts us by giving us a sense of belonging to Him and that we are no longer spiritual orphans. He becomes a Father to the fatherless, a Mother to the orphan, a Friend who is loyal and true and a Brother who never leaves us nor forsakes us.

He is the great Comforter whose presence brings perfect peace or Shalom. He comforts us with His reassuring peace.

Today, the world desperately needs peace. **So, the Holy Spirit is the Peace**. When we walk in the Holy Spirit, we abide in His perfect peace. He shelters us when we abide in His Comfort. He guards our minds and hearts from turmoil, inner turbulence, stress, worry and restlessness. He calms us down and gives us the strength to weather any storm and overcome it through His peace.

He comforts us with His word and His promises. **John 14:27 says," Peace I leave with you, my peace I give unto you: not as the world giveth, give I unto you. Let not your heart be troubled, neither let it be afraid."**

This scripture becomes a reality through the Comforter who is the Holy Ghost. When we receive the Comforter, we receive the Person of Peace. This peace which is given to us is the Holy Spirit because there is no peace apart from God. The Person of the Holy Spirit is the Spirit of Peace who protects our hearts from being troubled and fearful. He protects us from the tactics of the Devil who comes to attack our minds by giving us the mind of God instead.

We are engaged in a spiritual war and the war is against our minds. The enemy intentionally attacks our minds with fear, worry and torment so that we will be too distracted from serving God and living a victorious life in Christ. The Devil wants to steal our joy so we won't have the spiritual strength to walk in God's power and might.

He also attacks our minds so that we will live in a negative mindset and won't trust God and in His ability. He attacks our minds so that we will be depressed, feel hopeless and will stop speaking the word of God. Thus, he wars against our minds so that he can steal our testimonies of Christ.

The Holy Spirit comes to shield our minds with His peace, strength and comfort. He guards our hearts with His word, so that His word will be a light within us. He comes to comfort us that we are not alone, but God is with us. **Romans 14:17 says," For the kingdom of God is not meat and drink;**

but righteousness, and peace, and joy in the Holy Ghost. He brings the Kingdom of God within us and we have His righteousness, peace and joy." The Comforter comes to teach us all things. He teaches us about the kingdom of God and His kingdom benefits, He teaches us the word of God and brings understanding and revelations, He teaches us through His word. He teaches us through dreams and visions. He teaches us through His voice, inner promptings and unction. He teaches through His inward witness, holy word, and His ministers of truth. Whatever He teaches is always in alignment with the holy Bible. He never contradicts His word.

The Comforter also brings to our remembrance the word of God. Whatever Jesus has spoken, the Holy Spirit will confirm it. He reminds us of His promises, His word and what He has spoken. He will remind us to pray, seek His face and to study His word. He will remind us the things He has taught us so that we won't make the same mistakes again. He will also help us with natural things and remind us how to do things effectively and strategically. He will remind us of the promises and vows we have previously made to Him, so that we will implement it, keep it and walk in it.

He reminds us the word of God so that we will obey Him at all times and avoid pitfalls, not fall into disobedience, temptations and sin. He reminds us those things that He has taught us. He never forgets anything and He brings to our remembrance the things of God so that we will fulfill His plan on earth. He walks with us, teaches us, brings things to our remembrance and helps us to live a life of obedience to the word of God.

John 15:26 says," But when the Comforter is come, whom I will send unto you from the Father, even the Spirit of truth, which proceedeth from the Father, he shall testify of me:"

We again see in **John 15:26** that the Holy Spirit who is the Comforter came from the Heavenly Father. **He was sent to earth to testify of Jesus Christ. Thus, He testifies of the works of Jesus, words of Jesus and the finished work of the Cross.** Then, He also comforts us with the testimony of Jesus Christ, the finished work of the Cross and what Jesus has done for His church.

Holy Spirit is also our Helper and He helps us in all areas of our lives including our ministries and careers. He helps us to do the works of Jesus, speak the words of Jesus and walk in His mighty power. **He helps us in our weaknesses and in the areas we struggle in.** He empowers us and gives us His grace and strength to overcome them.

He helps us by guiding us, leading us, speaking to us, encouraging us and by being very patient with us. He helps us to walk in victory, in His grace and power. One of the ways He helps us is also by convicting us of our sins, giving us His grace to overcome weaknesses and temptations. He also helps us to walk in His truth through our obedience.

He is also referred to as the Spirit of Truth. It says in **1 John 4:6," We are of God: he that knoweth God heareth us; he that is not of God heareth not us. Hereby know we the spirit of truth, and the spirit of error."** Holy Spirit is Truth, Righteousness and Perfection. He came from the Heavenly

Father who is Holy, Purity and Righteous. Holy Spirit comforts us with His Truth, leads us in His Truth and teaches us the ways of truth and righteousness.

Holy Spirit or the Spirit of Truth can never speak a lie, can never make a mistake nor do anything contrary to His word. Spirit of God will never contradict the Heavenly Father and never do anything contrary to His will. He proceeded from the Heavenly Father and is intimately one with Him. He is also the Spirit of the Heavenly Father and carries the heart of the Abba, Father within Him. Thus, He is in perfect harmony with the Heavenly Father and His will, desires and order. He also testifies of the Heavenly Father and His Son Jesus Christ.

Holy Spirit is also one with Jesus Christ. He is in perfect agreement, harmony and alignment with His will, desires and order. The revelation of the Trinity is that They are three, yet They are perfectly One. Thus, They are eternally in perfect agreement with each other. They all have one will, one agreement and one exact order. They are perfectly equal to each other and are perfectly united. They never contradict each other and never work against each other.

Since the Holy Spirit is our Comforter and He came from the Heavenly Father, it demonstrates that the Heavenly Father is also our Comforter. He also gives us His peace made available to us through the shed blood and sufferings of Jesus Christ. Holy Spirit is God's comfort to us from the Heavenly Father. **Thus, the Comforter testifies of God's peace made available to us through the completed work of the Cross.**

Chapter 4
Ruach Elohim

Holy Spirit is also called the Spirit of God. He is referred to as **Ruach Elohim** in Hebrew or the Spirit of God. He is the Spirit of the Heavenly Father and is also the Spirit of Jesus Christ. He is God Himself.

The **Spirit of God is Omnipresent**. He is unlimited and eternal. He cannot be contained and limited by time, space or human logistics. His presence is limitless and He is omnipresent. **Space cannot contain Him, time cannot limit Him and human logistics cannot define Him.** He is Eternal and He has no beginning and no ending. God is a Spirit and He is an Unlimited God.

The **Spirit of God is Omnipotent**. He is the All Powerful God whose power is matchless. All universes are a result of His power. It was created as a result of His will. God the Father willed it, Jesus the Word spoke it and the Spirit of God manifested everything through His matchless power. It says in **Job 33:4,"The Spirit of God hath made me, and the breath of the Almighty hath given me life."** His power cannot be contained and it is uncontainable. His power holds the galaxies, planets and universes together and can never be exhausted. He anoints us with His power to become effective witnesses for Jesus Christ.

Even Jesus needed the anointing or the power of the Spirit of God to preach the gospel, heal the broken-hearted, to deliver the oppressed, cause the blind to see, to set at liberty those who are wounded and to preach the acceptable year of the Lord.

Luke 4:18- 19," The Spirit of the Lord is upon me, because he hath anointed me to preach the gospel to the poor; he hath sent me to heal the brokenhearted, to preach deliverance to the captives, and recovering of sight to the blind, to set at liberty them that are bruised, To preach the acceptable year of the Lord."

The Spirit of God is Omniscient. He knows all things at all times. There are seven billion people on earth, yet God knows all of their names, addresses and every detail about them all at the same time. There is nothing hidden from His eyes and He knows the thoughts of everyone simultaneously. He has countless angels working for Him who have different functions and responsibilities. It is so awesome that He knows them by their names as well.

Job 28:23-25 says," God understandeth the way thereof, and he knoweth the place thereof. For he looketh to the ends of the earth, and seeth under the whole heaven; To make the weight for the winds; and he weigheth the waters by measure."

Psalm 44:21 says," Shall not God search this out? for he knoweth the secrets of the heart."

Thus, Spirit of God is the Source of all wisdom, understanding, revelations and knowledge. He doesn't have to answer to anyone, consult anyone nor repent for anything because He is incapable of making a mistake. He can never do anything wrong. **He is His own Authority, and He is the Ultimate. He is the great Boss, He is the Lord, He**

is the Creator and He is God.

We must have the Spirit of God in us to ensure that we are saved and that we belong to Jesus Christ. We cannot receive Jesus without receiving His Spirit in us. When we invite Jesus Christ to come in our hearts, we are inviting the Spirit of Jesus to come within us. **Romans 8:9 says "But ye are not in the flesh, but in the Spirit, if so be that the Spirit of God dwell in you. Now if any man have not the Spirit of Christ, he is none of his."** Without the Holy Spirit we cannot be saved nor belong to Jesus Christ.

Our salvation is sealed by the Spirit of God. We must have the Holy Spirit who seals our salvation and guarantees that we are a child of God and that we have been engrafted in the family of Christ. Our redemption comes as a result of the work of the Spirit of God. He seals us in the blood of Jesus and makes us a citizen of the Kingdom of God. **Ephesians 4:30," And grieve not the holy Spirit of God, whereby ye are sealed unto the day of redemption."**

The Spirit of God knows the things of the Kingdom of God and the secrets of the Heavenly Father. Thus, through the Spirit of God we have the benefits of being sealed by Him. We receive the benefits of the Kingdom of God freely from the Holy Spirit.

We must understand that the Spirit of God is a Gift to us from Abba Father who brings the blessings of heaven to us. **1 Corinthians 2:11-12 says,"For what man knoweth the things of a man, save the spirit of man which is in him? even so the things of God knoweth no man, but the Spirit of God. Now we have received, not the spirit of the world, but the spirit which is of God; that we might know the things that are freely given to us of God."**

Besides salvation and receiving forgiveness for our sins, we also have the benefit of receiving the baptism of the Holy Spirit. Holy Spirit draws us to Jesus Christ, brings conviction of our sins and helps us to receive forgiveness for our sins. Then, when we get baptized in the Holy Spirit, we receive an overflow of the Spirit of God and His fire. We get endowed with His heavenly power.

We also receive an inward supernatural empowerment and a heavenly prayer language which is an evidence of the baptism of the Holy Spirit. **Matthew 3:16 says," And Jesus, when he was baptized, went up straightway out of the water: and, lo, the heavens were opened unto him, and he saw the Spirit of God descending like a dove, and lighting upon him:"**

Whenever the Spirit of God comes upon us there will be manifestations. The Spirit of God is not a dove but He is a Person of the Godhead. When He descended upon Jesus, He came upon Him like a dove and His presence manifested like a lightning upon Him. **When we get submerged in the Spirit of God, then the manifestation of that baptism is an overflow of His presence and power upon us**. The evidence of receiving the baptism of the Holy Spirit is the supernatural heavenly language.

The Spirit of God is a gift to us from the Heavenly Father. He also loves giving us gifts too. The Spirit of God gives us spiritual gifts and natural gifts. He decides our gifts, our callings and according to His will gives us His gifts for the purposes of building

His kingdom and serving others. **1 Corinthians 12:3-11-" Wherefore I give you to understand, that no man speaking by the Spirit of God calleth Jesus accursed: and that no man can say that Jesus is the Lord, but by the Holy Ghost. Now there are diversities of gifts, but the same Spirit. And there are differences of administrations, but the same Lord. And there are diversities of operations, but it is the same God which worketh all in all. But the manifestation of the Spirit is given to every man to profit withal. For to one is given by the Spirit the word of wisdom; to another the word of knowledge by the same Spirit; To another faith by the same Spirit; to another the gifts of healing by the same Spirit; To another the working of miracles; to another prophecy; to another discerning of spirits; to another divers kinds of tongues; to another the interpretation of tongues: But all these worketh that one and the selfsame Spirit, dividing to every man severally as he will."**

<u>The nine gifts of the Holy Spirit are:</u>

1) **Word of wisdom**- supernatural ability to solve complex problems through application of God's

word, revelations, divine instructions, supernatural ideas and supernatural wisdom. It can be given to us through supernatural means including dreams and visions.

2) **Word of knowledge**- attaining supernatural revelations or information of current or past situations, persons, places or events via supernatural means. God may reveal different sicknesses, healings and deliverances for the purpose of our redemption. Usually, multiple gifts of the Spirit tend to operate together. A person may feel heat, pain in certain parts of their body or certain emotions as God reveals the conditions of others who may be present at that time. God always reveals not to embarrass, but rather to bring redemption to the person.

3) **Gift of faith**- supernatural ability to believe and trust God for impossible situations to turn around, be resolved and become possible. Gift of faith is also the supernatural ability to boldly speak the word of God and see them manifest in the now. It is the supernatural ability to believe for a miracle and see it manifest in a supernatural way.

4) Gifts of healing- different streams of God's healing power for the healing of the spirit, soul, emotions and body. Supernatural manifestations of healing manifest when gifts of healing are in operation.

5) **Working of miracles**- creative miracles manifest, tangible creation of body parts which are absent or missing are created. It creates those things that were previously absent or missing. Supernatural, creative power of God that creates that which does not exist in the natural yet. The creation of missing organs, body parts and limbs are some of the examples of a creative miracle.

6) **Gift of prophecy**- divinely inspired utterances. It also includes those things that are yet to come and will manifest in the earth realm in God's timing. It is speaking the mysteries of God and declaring those things that are on the mind of God. It is speaking and declaring His plans, will and desires.

Though, it is God's will for everyone to prophesy. Having the gift of prophesy does not necessarily make someone a prophet, and is not the same as the office of the prophet. A prophet of God operates from the higher prophetic dimension and speaks as a mouthpiece of God.

They operate in the revelatory gifts, have the ability to cancel the plans of the devil, activate and also impart in others. They speak forth and cause the will of God to manifest in the earth realm. They stir up in others the gifts of the Holy Spirit. They also speak the word of God and then see them manifest in the natural.

7) **Discerning of spirits**- supernatural ability to look beyond the natural and know that which is hidden, concealed and not revealed. The supernatural ability to know genuine moves and workings of God. It is also the ability to see in the heavenly realm, know the manifestations of demonic spirits, angelic activities and also know the motives, intentions of a human spirit.

8) **Divers kinds of tongues**- supernatural ability to speak in heavenly languages to deliver messages from God or speak in earthly languages never previously learned. It delivers to the body of Christ a message from God.

9) **Interpretation of tongues**- supernatural ability to interpret and deliver messages from God in a known language after a message has been delivered in the heavenly tongues.

Though there are diversities of gifts, differences of administrations and diversities of operations yet it is the same Spirit of God behind them and He is the one who brings forth manifestations. He is the one who decides what gifts to give to each one us and He administers His gifts differently to each one of us according to His will. He places His gifts within us and wants us to flow in the gifts of the Holy Spirit for the purposes of building His kingdom and the body of Christ.

The Spirit of God uses everyone differently and His operations are different through each one of us. We need to discern how He chooses to operate through us. For example, someone with a prophetic gift may be used by the Spirit of God through their prophetic dance, another may prophesy through their prophetic songs.

One may be called to be a prophetic intercessor and that prophetic gift may operate while they are praying and interceding. The Lord may give them prophetic decrees and declarations to speak over nations or individuals. On the other hands, others may prophesy when prophetic unction comes upon them. Some may see in the realm of the Holy Spirit, while someone else may hear the voice of God speaking to them. Thus, it is the same Spirit of God, but how He operates through an individual depends upon the will of the Holy Spirit.

Receiving the Baptism of the Holy Spirit

1) Pray this prayer – "**Heavenly Father, I repent of all of my sins. Forgive me and wash me with the precious blood of Jesus. I receive Lord Jesus Christ as my Lord and Savior. I believe that He died on the cross for my sins and rose from the dead. I ask You to baptize me in your Holy Spirit and fire in Jesus' name. I receive Your Holy Spirit and the baptism of fire with the evidence of praying in the heavenly language. I welcome You Holy Spirit. Immerse me now in Your Holy Spirit so that I will overflow with Your power and presence. I submit and surrender my life to You now. I want to thank You for my heavenly prayer language. I receive it in Jesus' name. Amen.**"

2) Tell the believer that the Holy Spirit is a Gift from the Heavenly Father who has already been given to us. All we have to do now is to receive the precious Gift of the Holy

Spirit and be immersed in Him .Convey that the Holy Spirit is Almighty God and He is a Person. All we have to do is to receive Him.

3) Tell him that He is the One who makes Jesus real to us. Through repentance, we are ready for this precious Gift of God.

4) Tell the believer that the evidence of the baptism of the Holy Spirit and being immersed in Him is speaking in tongues or the heavenly language. This is received by faith. **Acts 2:4 says," And they were all filled with the Holy Ghost, and began to speak with other tongues, as the Spirit gave them utterance."** It also says in **Ephesians 5:18, "And be not drunk with wine, wherein is excess, but be filled with the Spirit."**

5) Lay your hands on the head of the believer and pray. Then tell the believer to exercise his faith by opening his mouth and to speak. As he does that, the Holy Spirit will give him

words to speak which will make no sense to his mind.

6) Tell the believer to take a step of faith and boldly speak, as the Holy Spirit will give Him words in the heavenly language.

7) Encourage the believer to continue exercising his heavenly prayer language, even though it may be a word or couple of words or a sentence. The more he prays in the heavenly language, the more the Lord will continue increasing his prayer vocabulary.

Chapter 5

Demonstrations of the Anointing

The gospel of Jesus Christ must be demonstrated through the power of God. Every time we minister the word of God, it must be accompanied **by signs, wonders and miracles.** We must not just tell people that Jesus is alive but we must show them that Jesus Christ is alive. I have learned that the love of God must be demonstrated through the anointing of the Holy Spirit.

Today, all across the world many leaders with charisma preach a nice, feel good message. But, there are no demonstrations of God's power. Thus, people leave the church the same way they first walked in. They come in with bondages and leave with the same demons that continue to torment and harass them.

Sadly, many people tend to confuse charisma, hype, charm and being polished with the anointing. They think that hype is the anointing. So they sing some songs, jump and shout and are satisfied with it. Thus, ignorance destroys them and produces no inner transformation. Sadly, many people have never experienced the raw, supernatural power of God.

It says in **1 Corinthians 2:4-5," And my speech and my preaching was not with enticing words of man's wisdom, but in demonstration of the Spirit and of power: That your faith should not stand in the wisdom of men, but in the power of God."**

We clearly see in the above scriptures that Apostle Paul's speech and preaching was not with enticing words of man's wisdom. Rather, it was born from the Holy Spirit being backed up with the demonstrations of His power and divine ability. Thus, we must also learn this lesson by demonstrating the power of God each time we preach the word of God to others.

We must never preach a message on healing without demonstrating the healing power of God. Or on deliverance without seeing its manifestations. The word of God must be confirmed with signs, wonders and miracles. Today, many leaders do not give room to the Holy Spirit to minister to His people through the power of God. Thus, many leaders are guilty of grieving and quenching the move of the Holy Spirit. That is an insult to the leadership of the Holy Spirit. They also restrict the Holy Spirit by preparing an intellectual message from their heads, rather than the leading of the Holy Spirit.

The five enemies of the power of God are 1) intellectualism- man's wisdom and human logics 2) man's traditions 3) the religious spirit 4) carnality and 5) lack of intimacy with the Holy Spirit. These five enemies must be defeated so that we can experience the power of God in an unrestricted manner and experience open heavens.

I believe that the secret to moving in the supernatural power of the Holy Spirit is intimacy with the Holy Spirit. **The revelation I want to impart to you is that the intimacy with the Holy Spirit produces sensitivity to His voice.** When we respond to His voice through obedience, then we will experience supernatural manifestations.

Intimacy with the Holy Spirit also requires being hungry and thirsty for His presence. God can only fill us with **more**, is when we become hungry and thirsty for Him. **Another revelation I want to impart in you is that the greater your hunger, greater will be your capacity to receive even a deeper infilling of His Holy Spirit.**

Bishop Arnold Gajramsingh shared with me some of the spiritual keys concerning intimacy with the Holy Spirit. He stated," First of all you must develop both thirst and hunger for the Holy Spirit." He explained to me the importance of it. Then, he also said that his best experiences in the Holy Spirit are when he is all alone and by himself. Thus, having personal and intimate times with the Holy Spirit are very important. Also, when we pray in our heavenly language we are accessing greater dimensions.

Bishop Arnold Gajramsingh further stated," the Holy Spirit is like a wind and you can feel the wind blowing over your face, over your body. It will make you want to worship Him more, reach out to others more and develop more compassion and humility." He went on to say that being chosen by the Holy Spirit is a priveledge, so that we can empower the lives of others.

I also personally believe that we need to have an intimacy with the Holy Spirit so that we can receive fresh anointing and new revelations daily. We cannot live on yesterday's anointing. Thus, we must get in His presence daily, in order to receive from the Holy Spirit on a daily basis.

Intimacy with the Holy Spirit requires from us being obedient to Him. The only way we can please the Holy Spirit is by obeying Him and doing what He tells us to do. **Obedience is our love language to the Holy Spirit.** Our honor for the Holy Spirit must be demonstrated through our obedience to His word.

When we honor the Holy Spirit then it will be easier for us to honor others around us. **When we honor the Holy Spirit through obedience then we will also honor our bodies, which is His temple.** Then, we will take care of our bodies and not abuse it nor mistreat it.

Our relationship with the Holy Spirit will impact all areas of our lives. **Our relationships with others will become healthier, more wholesome and will have longevity.** Obedience to the Holy Spirit will bring supernatural blessings upon our lives and we will experience open heavens. We will also experience the blessings of the Lord in the area of our finances as we honor the Holy Spirit through our obedience.

Intimacy with the Holy Spirit will make us supernatural worshippers. **When we create an atmosphere for His presence through praise and worship, then we will host His manifested glory.** We must make it a habit on a daily basis to intentionally create an atmosphere to host His presence and intimately encounter Him. Wherever His manifested glory is, there the supernatural power of God is also manifested.

Intimacy with the Holy Spirit produces the leadership of the Holy Spirit in our lives. Then His leadership always produces supernatural demonstrations of His mighty power. It causes the name of Jesus Christ to be consistently glorified and magnified.

Thus, we must always lean and submit to the Holy Spirit. We must ask for His wisdom and guidance on a regular basis. We must become God seekers through intimacy with Him on a daily basis. That must be our desire and our lifestyle.

Chapter 6
Ruach Elohim Chayim

In Hebrew, the **Spirit of the Living God** is called **Ruach Elohim Chayim.** He is a Living God who is alive and has never known nor experienced death. Holy Spirit is the Living God. We don't serve a dead, lifeless God nor do we serve a God of yesterday. Out of the Living God, proceeded the Living Spirit of God. He brings life and is the Author of Life.

Since, He is Alive and Living, He is the One who raised Jesus from the dead. He is also the Resurrection power of God. Our Lord Jesus is alive and seated next to the Heavenly Father. He sent His Spirit on earth to draw all men to Jesus Christ and to bring them into an intimate relationship with Jesus Christ.

2 Corinthians 3:3 "Forasmuch as ye are manifestly declared to be the epistle of Christ ministered by us, written not with ink, but with the Spirit of the living God; not in tables of stone,

but in fleshy tables of the heart." It is by the Ruach Elohim Chayim that we have been manifestly declared to be a testimony of what the power of God can do. Many of us were lost in darkness but it is the Spirit of the Living God who rescued us from the hands of Satan and brought us into the marvelous light of God's Kingdom. Thus, we became a witness for Christ and our story has been written by the **Ruach Elohim Chayim**. Our testimony should point others to Jesus Christ and glorify Him at all times. It says in **Revelation 19:10," And I fell at his feet to worship him. And he said unto me, See thou do it not: I am thy fellowservant, and of thy brethren that have the testimony of Jesus: worship God: for the testimony of Jesus is the spirit of prophecy."**

It is the Spirit of the Living God who makes our testimony effective and gives it the ability to touch hearts. He brings conviction of sin and melts stony hearts and turns them into hearts of flesh that can feel His presence and respond to it. He has the ability to bring inner transformation and change of mindsets. He is the One who ignites the fire of passion and causes it to burn from within. **Thus, inner transformation is not the result of what is on the outside but rather due to the One who lives within us.**

Ruach Elohim Chayim causes revival to manifest, as His manifest glory brings heaven on earth. He brings life of the Spirit to manifest where there is dryness, barrenness and spiritual death. He brings laughter, peace, love, happiness and salvation where there is chaos, depression, turmoil and separation. He causes hearts to be turned to Jesus Christ again and passion for God to manifest. He causes repentance to happen and for people to seek the face of God. Thus, revival brings spiritual healing, restoration and transformation.

We are living in the hour of the outpouring of the Former and Latter Rain of the Holy Spirit. The flood of His manifested glory will cover the earth as the Spirit of the Living God moves in an unprecedented way. There will be a gushing and an overflow of His presence through yielded vessels who have submitted themselves totally to the Holy Spirit.

The outpouring of the former and latter rain of the Holy Spirit will produce the **great harvest** of souls who are hungry and desperate for the Living God. **The outpouring will produce spiritual awakening and many sleeping giants will be awakened who would burn passionately with the fire of God.** They would be lovers of God who will choose Him above the pleasures of the flesh and the world.

We have the promise of the outpouring of the Holy Spirit in **Joel 2:28-31, "And it shall come to pass afterward, that I will pour out my spirit upon all flesh; and your sons and your daughters shall prophesy, your old men shall dream dreams, your young men shall see visions. And also upon the servants and upon the handmaids in those days will I pour out my spirit. And I will shew wonders in the heavens and in the earth, blood, and fire, and pillars of smoke. The sun shall be turned into darkness, and the moon into blood, before the great and the terrible day of the lord come."** We are seeing this happen now. This outpouring of the Holy Spirit will bring a great harvest of souls who will choose Jesus, enter the Kingdom of God and repent of their sinful ways.

I prophesy that the Holy Spirit will tremendously touch the youth of this generation. He is raising a new army of young people who will carry the fire of God. They will be bold and courageous, declaring the word of God and demonstrating the power of the Holy Spirit. They will shake nations and bring transformations through the power of God. They will come from various backgrounds, different cultures, nationalities and from all age groups.

The Spirit of God will draw them to Jesus despite where they have been and the situations they have encountered. He will take them and transform them inwardly. He will anoint them with His mighty power and use them in a powerful way.

Also, there will be a dramatic increase of the supernatural visitations of the Holy Spirit in dreams, visions and God encounters. There will be unusual manifestations of the power of God with uncommon demonstrations of His manifested glory.

Hosea 6:2-3 says, "After two days will he revive us; in the third day he will raise us up, and we

shall live in his sight. Then shall we know, if we follow on to know the Lord: his going forth is prepared as the morning; and he shall come unto us as the rain, as the latter and former rain unto the earth."

This outpouring of the rain of the Holy Spirit will bring renewal and refreshment from the throne of God. **Acts 3:19 says, "Repent ye therefore, and be converted, that your sins may be blotted out, when the times of refreshing shall come from the presence of God;"** Many who are dry from within and have lost the fire of passion for Him will experience inner transformations and revival as they repent and intimately receive from being in the presence of God. But they must go and choose to be where the outpouring of the Holy Spirit is and not where religious minds reject the rain of the Holy Spirit.

They must be hungry and thirsty for the rain of God and not comfortable and complacent with just a Sunday church mentality. They must be willing to encounter God in new ways and be willing to give up man's traditions and ideology that wants to restrict God and place Him in a box.

Traditions of men works against the moves of the Holy Spirit which desires to confine God and limit Him. It says in **Mark 7:13," Making the word of God of none effect through your tradition, which ye have delivered: and many such like things do ye."** Thus, the Holy Spirit is quenched by many who restrict the working of the Holy Spirit by not allowing Him to flow in the way He desires. The carnal nature wants to take over and is not flexible to the move of the Holy Spirit. Thus, many are more interested in man-made programs today which lacks the presence of God.

Joel 2:23-26 says," Be glad then, ye children of Zion, and rejoice in the Lord your God: for he hath given you the former rain moderately, and he will cause to come down for you the rain, the former rain, and the latter rain in the first month. And the floors shall be full of wheat, and the vats shall overflow with wine and oil. And I will restore to you the years that the locust hath eaten, the cankerworm, and the caterpillar, and the palmerworm, my great army which I sent

among you. And ye shall eat in plenty, and be satisfied, and praise the name of the Lord your God, that hath dealt wondrously with you: and my people shall never be ashamed."

In the above scripture, the **wine represents** the Holy Spirit who lives within us. He is the Anointing who lives within us and teaches us all things. Thus, the wine of the Holy Spirit within us is also for our relationship with Him and to host His presence within.

Then the **oil represents** the Holy Spirit upon us and His grace that covers us. The oil upon us is for our calling and purpose. It is also for our ministry office. It rests upon our ministry and for us to be effective in the call of God.

The **wheat represents** the living word of God that reveals Jesus to us. Thus, the outpouring of the Holy Spirit brings an increase of the presence of God within us as we hunger and thirst for Him and strengthens our walk with God. It increases the unction of the Holy Spirit upon us and makes us to operate in the supernatural power of God as we walk in the revelations of Jesus is. He manifests

Himself to us in a greater way through His word, revelations and God encounters.

The **rain of the Spirit of God brings lightning with it.** The lightning of God brings the fire of God. It brings radiance, illumination and passion for God. **Habakkuk 3:4 says," And his brightness was as the light; he had horns coming out of his hand: and there was the hiding of his power."** Then the rain of God also represents the blessings of God coming down as we receive in reverence the precious Holy Spirit. **When we honor the presence of the Holy Spirit and respect Him, we will also receive His rain of blessings upon our lives.**

Wherever the rain of the Spirit of God is, there is also His clouds. **His clouds represents His manifested glory.** The glory of God is God Himself, manifesting to us. Wherever the rain of the Holy Spirit is, there His wind is also present. **The very nature of the Holy Spirit is to move like a wind.** He moves very suddenly and like a wind causes movement. **Exodus 15:8 says," And with the blast of thy nostrils the waters were gathered together, the floods stood upright as an heap,**

and the depths were concealed in the heart of the sea."

The rain of the Holy Spirit will cause:

1) Inner awakenings and an inward revival.
2) Passion for God and hunger for Him.
3) He will draw us closer to Jesus and cause us to walk in a greater intimacy with Him.
4) It will bring the blessings of God upon us and our families. It will bring the knowledge of His glory and cause His manifested glory to be revealed in our lives.
5) We will have His abiding presence within us and we will experience the supernatural moves of God in our lives.
6) We will experience His supernatural power and He will cause us to do what we have never done before.
7) We will experience a gushing overflow of His power and presence from within us.
8) We will walk in victory and open heavens.
9) We will experience restoration in all areas of our lives.
10) We will never be ashamed.

11) We will receive deeper revelations of Jesus Christ.

12) We will receive fresh anointing of the Holy Spirit.

In order to experience the glorious rain of the Holy Spirit, we must live a life of repentance. We will have to make a commitment to the Holy Spirit to love Him, honor Him, obey Him, trust Him and serve Him. We must allow the Holy Spirit to transform us from within and help us to relinquish our will and desires for the purposes of following His will for our lives.

We must repent from all iniquities, sins, dead and unfruitful works of the carnal flesh. We must be willing to crucify the works, deeds and the nature of the carnal flesh which works in contrary to the will and the nature of the Holy Spirit.

We must be willing to pray, intercede in the Holy Ghost, and seek the face of God daily. We must learn to wait on the Lord and honor Him through waiting on Him. Our flesh is very impatient and wants everything now. One of the ways to crucify our flesh is by learning to wait on God, wait for His timing and for His manifested presence.

We must learn to become desperate for God and willing to respond to His presence. **Today, many people lack desperation for His presence. They are satisfied with singing one or two songs, hearing a nice message and then going home. That is not desperation for God.** Desperation for God is being willing to wait on God with a hungry heart regardless of how long it takes for God to reveal Himself and manifest His presence. Then, being willing to respond to His presence by being sensitive to His needs and wants. This is very important for cultivating an intimate relationship with the Holy Spirit.

We must be willing to pay the price by becoming an offering at the holy altar of God. We must become intimate worshippers who know how to create an atmosphere through our worship to host His manifest presence. Holy Spirit loves worship, He responds to heartfelt songs and He loves to come and commune with us. We must worship the Holy Spirit daily. **2 Corinthians 13:14 says," The grace of the Lord Jesus Christ, and the**

love of God, and the communion of the Holy Ghost, be with you all. Amen."

We must be willing to fellowship with the Holy Spirit and talk to Him on a daily basis. Our fellowship with the Holy Spirit must produce in us the mind of Christ and the willingness to walk in unity with His word. He loves to fellowship with us and He loves being a friend to us. **Philippians 2:1 says," If there be therefore any consolation in Christ, if any comfort of love, if any fellowship of the Spirit, if any bowels and mercies, Fulfil ye my joy, that ye be likeminded, having the same love, being of one accord, of one mind."**

We must willingly and lovingly celebrate His presence by abiding in Him. Abiding in Him produces the nature of Christ in us and equips us to do the works of Jesus. **Galatians 5:22-23 says, " But the fruit of the Spirit is love, joy, peace, longsuffering, gentleness, goodness, faith, meekness, temperance: against such there is no law."** We become witnesses for Christ by not just what we say, but how we live our lives on a daily basis. Thus, when we bear the fruit of the Spirit, then we will reflect Christ through us.

We must be willing to live a life of obedience to the word and the voice of the Holy Spirit. We must always be willing to follow His leadership. We must also have listening ears to His voice, be intimately tuned to Him so we can recognize His whispers. We must be sensitive when He bears inward witness with our spirit. We must recognize His promptings and be obedient to His instructions. **Hebrews 5:8 says," Though he were a Son, yet learned he obedience by the things which he suffered; And being made perfect, he became the author of eternal salvation unto all them that obey him;"** Jesus lived a life of obedience to His Heavenly Father. We too must live a life of obedience by obeying the voice of God at all times.

We must walk in the revelation that we are sons and daughters of the Living God and we must **daily cry out Abba, Father**. We must change our mentalities and believe that we are no longer spiritual orphans and we have not been rejected by God.

Many people have difficulty cultivating an intimate relationship with God because they have an orphan mentality and feel very unworthy to approach the throne of God. **Yet, Holy Spirit is the One who bears witness with our spirit that we are the children of God** and we have the right to boldly approach His throne of grace. He assures us that we have the right to receive the promises of God. **Romans 8:15-16 says," For ye have not received the spirit of bondage again to fear; but ye have received the Spirit of adoption, whereby we cry, Abba, Father. The Spirit itself beareth witness with our spirit, that we are the children of God."**

We must also be willing to walk in the healthy fear of the Lord. This requires for us to hate sin and embrace holiness and purity. **Proverbs 8:13 says," The fear of the Lord is to hate evil: pride, and arrogancy, and the evil way, and the forward mouth, do I hate."**

The Holy Spirit is also the **Spirit of Holiness**. Thus, walking in holiness is not an option but it is a necessity and required by the Lord God. Holy Spirit is a gift from God to us and He renews, transforms and changes us to become holy. **Romans 1:4 says," And declared to be the Son of**

God with power, according to the spirit of holiness, by the resurrection from the dead."

Chapter 7

The Holy Spirit's Purpose for Us

God created each and every one of us with a purpose. In order for us to be able to complete God's purpose for our lives, He gave us a Helper whose name is the Holy Spirit. We see in John 16 where Jesus was telling His disciples how important it was for Him to leave them so He can send us a Helper. **John 16:6-12 "Nevertheless I tell you the truth; It is expedient for you that I go away: for if I go not away, the Comforter will not come unto you; but if I depart, I will send him unto you. And when he is come, he will reprove the world of sin, and of righteousness, and of judgment: Of sin, because they believe not on me, Of righteousness, because I go to my Father, and ye see me no more; Of judgment, because the prince of this world is judged. I have yet many things to say unto you, but ye cannot bear them now."**

Jesus knew that His disciple would not be able to complete their God given assignment if the Holy Spirit was not with them. For example, Peter denied Jesus three times when He was taken to be crucified for us, **Mark 14:66-72 "And as Peter was beneath in the palace, there cometh one of** the maids of the high priest: And when she saw Peter warming himself, she looked upon him, and said, And thou also wast with Jesus of Nazareth. But he denied, saying, I know not, neither understand I what thou sayest. And he went out into the porch; and the cock crew. And a maid saw him again, and began to say to them that stood by, This is one of them. And he denied it again. And a little after, they that stood by said again to Peter, Surely thou art one of them: for thou art a Galilaean, and thy speech agreeth thereto. But he began to curse and to swear, saying, I know not this man of whom ye speak. And the second time the cock crew. And Peter called to mind the word that Jesus said unto him, Before the cock crow twice, thou shalt deny me thrice. And when he thought thereon, he wept."

A few chapters later, Peter defended Jesus among the same group of people and even greater stature of men with boldness and with no fear of been persecuted by men. What was the difference? What cause Peter to gain such boldness? Let see **Acts2:2-24**·" And suddenly there came a sound from heaven as of a rushing mighty wind, and it filled all the house where they were sitting. And there appeared unto them cloven tongues like as of fire, and it sat upon each of them. And they were all filled with the Holy Ghost, and began to speak with other tongues, as the Spirit gave them utterance. And there were dwelling at Jerusalem Jews, devout men, out of every nation under heaven. Now when this was noised abroad, the multitude came together, and were confounded, because that every man heard them speak in his own language. And they were all amazed and marvelled, saying one to another, Behold, are not all these which speak Galilaeans? And how hear we every man in our own tongue, wherein we were born?

Parthians, and Medes, and Elamites, and the dwellers in Mesopotamia, and in Judaea, and Cappadocia, in Pontus, and Asia, Phrygia, and Pamphylia, in Egypt, and in the parts of Libya about Cyrene, and strangers of Rome, Jews and proselytes, Cretes and Arabians, we do hear them speak in our tongues the wonderful works of God. And they were all amazed, and were in doubt, saying one to another, What meaneth this? Others mocking said, These men are full of new wine. But Peter, standing up with the eleven, lifted up his voice, and said unto them, Ye men of Judaea, and all ye that dwell at Jerusalem, be this known unto you, and hearken to my words: For these are not drunken, as ye suppose, seeing it is but the third hour of the day. But this is that which was spoken by the prophet Joel; And it shall come to pass in the last days, saith God, I will pour out of my Spirit upon all flesh: and your sons

and your daughters shall prophesy, and your young men shall see visions, and your old men shall dream dreams: And on my servants and on my handmaidens I will pour out in those days of my Spirit; and they shall prophesy: And I will shew wonders in heaven above, and signs in the earth beneath; blood, and fire, and vapour of smoke: The sun shall be turned into darkness, and the moon into blood, before the great and notable day of the Lord come: And it shall come to pass, that whosoever shall call on the name of the Lord shall be saved. Ye men of Israel, hear these words; Jesus of Nazareth, a man approved of God among you by miracles and wonders and signs, which God did by him in the midst of you, as ye yourselves also know: Him, being delivered by the determinate counsel and foreknowledge of God, ye have taken, and by wicked hands have crucified and slain: Whom God hath raised up, having loosed the pains of death: because it was not possible that he should be holden of it." Here we see a spirit of boldness that came upon Peter after he had received the gift of the Holy Ghost. No of us can effectively pray, minister the word of God, or do any do the work of God without the Holy Spirit.

1. **The Holy Spirit teaches us all things.**
    a. **John 14:26** "But the Comforter, which is the Holy Ghost, whom the Father will send in my name, he shall

teach you all things, and bring all things to your remembrance, whatsoever I have said unto you."

2. **He convicts us.**
    a. John16:8 " And when he is come, he will reprove the world of sin, and of righteousness, and of judgment:"
3. **He empowers us to be witnesses for our Lord Jesus Christ.**
    a. John 15:26 "But when the Comforter is come, whom I will send unto you from the Father, even the Spirit of truth, who proceedeth from the Father, He shall testify of Me."

    b. Acts 1:8 "But ye shall receive power, after the Holy Ghost is come upon you: and ye shall be witnesses unto me both in Jerusalem, and in all Judea, and in Samaria, and unto the uttermost part of the earth."

    c. Acts 4:33 And with great power gave the apostles witness of the resurrection of the Lord Jesus. And great grace was upon them all.

    d. 1 Corinthians 2:4-5 And my speech and my preaching was not with enticing words of man's wisdom, but in demonstration of the Spirit and of power, that your faith should not stand in the wisdom of men, but in the power of God.

4. **He comforts us.**
    a. **Acts 9:31** "Then had the churches rest throughout all Judaea and Galilee and Samaria, and were edified; and walking in the fear of the Lord, and in the comfort of the Holy Ghost, were multiplied.

5. **He gives us spiritual gifts for the edification of believers.**

6. **He is our guarantee of eternal life with God.**
    a. 2 Corinthians 1:21-22 Now He who establishes us with you in Christ, and hath anointed us, is God; Who hath also sealed us, and given the earnest of the Spirit in our hearts.
    b. **Ephesians 1:13-14 "In whom ye also trusted, after that ye heard the word of truth, the gospel of your salvation: in whom also after that ye believed, ye were sealed with that holy Spirit of promise, Which is the earnest of our inheritance until the**

redemption of the purchased possession, unto the praise of his glory."
7. **He helps us to remember the word of God.**
   a. **John 14:26 " But the Comforter, *which is* the Holy Ghost, whom the Father will send in my name, he shall teach you all things, and bring all things to your remembrance, whatsoever I have said unto you."**

Matthew 3:16 "And Jesus, when he was baptized, went up straightway out of the water: and, lo, the heavens were opened unto him, and he saw the Spirit of God descending like a dove, and lighting upon him:"

If Jesus our Lord and Savior needed the Holy Spirit for His assignment on earth, how much more us.

In order for the Holy Spirit to manifest His purpose in our lives we need to have a relationship with Him. We need to spend extensive times in praising, thanking, worshiping, reading and meditating on His word, and communing with Him. The more we spent time in His presence, our spiritual senses will increase and we will discern and know His leading. We will understand that the Holy Spirit is a Person; He thinks, feels, makes decisions and has a personality.

One Saturday in year 2012, I was home relaxing and planning a quite Sunday to stay home from service because I did not have gas in my vehicle neither did I have money to buy gas. An elder from my home church called to let me know she needed me to teach Sunday class for the children's ministry. As I was about to tell her I could not attend service, the Holy Spirit unctioned me to say "yes". I did as the Holy Spirit unctioned me to do, trusting that God will provide the gas money by Sunday morning.

Then, Sunday morning came and no one had blessed me with the gas money for my 63 miles journey to church. At first I was a little worried, then the Holy Spirit reminded me that He told me to accept the assignment and to trust Him. I got in my vehicle, looked at the gas gage and it was still on empty. I prayed, started up my vehicle and started on my 63 miles journey to church.

While trying to block all the negative thoughts I was having, I turned on my worship music and began to worship God as I drove. A few miles into driving I heard the empty gas signal over the music and heard in my spirit "You are now driving on faith". I began to cry at how amazing God is. I made it to church on an empty tank of gas driving over 63 miles. During the service the Holy Spirit told someone to bless me with $25.00. I was again able to drive the empty tank of gas to the gas station where I then purchased gas to get back home. From this experience, my faith has increased in the things of God and to trust in the leading of the Holy Spirit.

When the Holy Spirit unction us to do something, He will not show or tell us the beginning through the end. We have to trust Him and know that His ways will steer us best, even when it doesn't make sense in the natural. The more we spend time in His presence, the more we get to learn when He is speaking to us.

I talk to Him first thing in the morning. I welcome Him into my day and ask Him to direct my path. Sometimes, He will reschedule my day. I might not like it but I know it is for the best. He might tell me to stop what I am doing and pray for a specific person. Later, I would find out that the individual the Holy Spirit had asked me to pray for was having a rough day. As a result of my obedience to pray, his situation changed for the better. At other times, the Holy Spirit has unctioned me to pray and bind up the spirit of death off a person's life. Later on that day, I learned that the person was in a car accident but was not hurt. Holy Spirit always honors our acts of obedience.

Sometimes the Holy Spirit will warn us of upcoming life changing events in our lives. I can remember in February of 2015, my mom had been through a brain surgery. I was fasting and praying for her recovery when the Holy Spirit spoke to me and told me to stop praying for her healing because she wanted to come home. I remember weeping so hard and I said "Help me Lord. She is my friend, my mother and my biggest supporter". "I will miss her." The peace of God came and overwhelmed me. I wiped my tears and began to thank God for giving me forty nine years with her and choosing her to be my mother. Then the Holy Spirit told me I had three more days with her. During those three days I made sure all the close family members spoke with her and as the Holy Spirit had said she went home to be with the Lord on the third day.

My family member could not understand how I was at peace and was not crying and was not being frantic. Thanks be to the Holy Spirit for warning me and giving me peace. I often have said that the Holy Spirit is my friend. I talk to Him all the time and pay attention to what He is saying to me. Simple things like when I misplaced my car key, I would ask Him to tell me where it is and He always does.

Before making any decisions in life, I would ask Him for His ideas. Most of us would not recognize His leading because we don't spend time worshiping, praying and meditating on His word. We have to be still in His presence to hear Him as He speaks. You would be amazed of the things you hear when you listen to His voice.

When we speak to a friend on the phone whom we cannot see, yet we know who we are talking to and we know their voice. Why is it so? We discern who that person is because we have spent time with them, have built a relationship with them and know their voice. Similarly, when we spend time with the Holy Spirit, we will know His voice and His leading. Intimacy is the key to the heart of the Holy Spirit.

<u>Outpouring of the Holy Spirit</u>

I believe we are in a season of life where we are beginning to see a supernatural outpouring of the Holy Spirit. The prophetic words from the Lord tells us that He will pour out His Spirit on ALL FLESH. God did not say some, **He said ALL**, and therefore we need to position ourselves so that we can maximize the anointing He will pour out on us.

<u>Acts 2:17</u> "And it shall come to pass in the last days, saith God, I will pour out of my Spirit upon all flesh: and your sons and your daughters shall prophesy, and your young men shall see visions, and your old men shall dream dreams:"

<u>Joel 2:28</u> "And it shall come to pass afterward, *that* I will pour out my spirit upon all flesh; and your sons and your daughters shall prophesy, your old men shall dream dreams, your young men shall see visions:

<u>Isaiah 44:3-4</u> "For I will pour water upon him that is thirsty, and floods upon the dry ground: I will pour my spirit upon thy seed, and my blessing upon thine offspring: And they shall

spring up *as* among the grass, as willows by the water courses."

We will see evidence of us having more dreams and visions from the Holy Spirit. The Lord uses me to teach Dreams and Visions classes. I have seen so many people who have never dreamed nor could remember their dreams go through this class and begun to have dreams and visions. They also began remembering their dreams and visions.

As I prayed and the Lord would activate them, I have seen the manifestation of the Lord giving them the interpretation of their dreams. God is true to His word, He would not say it and don't do it if we listen to His word and believe it. We need to live a life of righteousness and holiness. We need to live a life of repentance, daily asking God to forgive us of our sins and change anything within us that displeases the Lord.

As ministers of the gospel, we should not compromise the word of God. We should at all times worship Him in Spirit and in truth. Allow His spirit to flow in and through us. Be obedient to His leading even when it does not make any sense to us. Trust the Holy Spirit's guidance at all times.

We are seeing more and more of how God is releasing the Spirit of Prophecy in our services. This is another sign of the beginning stages of Him pouring out His Spirit on all flesh. God is not only using the Prophets to prophecy, but He is releasing the Spirit of Prophecy on all those who seek Him, those who are truly worshiping Him and have a hunger for Him.

We will begin to see unusual and unexpected moves of God in our lives, homes, churches, cities and nations. God will do things that doesn't make sense to the natural mind. His supernatural manifestations will be the norm in our daily life. The Holy Spirit will impart a higher dimension of power, anointing and faith in our lives. We are to stand in a prayerful position at all times. God is calling the intercessors for our families, our churches, our ministries, our cities, and our nations to arise and be all that God has called them to be.

In January of 2017, I received a prophetic word that the Lord desires for me to shut down everything that I am doing in the natural and be in His presence on a specific day and time. I did as I was told. During my time of waiting, I praised, thanked and worshiped the Lord. A few minutes later, I was caught up in a vision. I was walking in a large white room wearing a white gown with angels there, and the Lord's disciples including Apostle Paul were present there. There were others also whom I didn't recognize. But Lord Jesus was present there. As I marched in the room, as if I was in a graduation ceremony and they were cheering me on.

I was the only person graduating. They all cheered at me with the look of gratitude. I saw the Lord smiling and I marched towards this unique altar where He was standing. It did not look like the altars in our churches. As I stood before Him, He placed a crown with bright crystals on my head. The Lord then instructed me to never get in a discussion about any Pastors' flaws. The Lord said to me "I am giving you dominion over Nations." As I thought, what about United States of America? He responded "and all of USA, my daughter, be careful what you speak over people's lives and nations because it will manifest".

The Lord also gave me a sword among other things and commanded me to use it. As the vision ended, I was left with a strong presence of God and a feeling of drunkenness. In my spirit, I understood, but in the natural I did not completely comprehend it until several weeks later. As I was interceding for someone whom I saw in the spirit, demonic spirits surrounded her. I pulled the sword without realizing what I was doing and began to slay then. Within seconds the multitude of demonic spirits were defeated.

If you saw me in the natural I looked foolish, but praise be to God, the person I was praying for gained victory. There was also the manifestation of victory in the natural in her life. When the Holy Spirit leads us to do things, it will not make sense at the time. We have to trust the Holy Spirit and know that He has our best interest for our lives. He will equip us for the assignment He has for us to complete. Many of us have been in preparation for years and He is saying the time is now for unfulfilled promises, purposes, callings, visions, dreams, prayers and prophecies to come to pass.

The Lord gave me a vision over five years ago that He will use my hands to heal the sick, and raise the dead. I thought it was strange because at that time I taught business classes and had nothing to do with the ministry of healing and deliverance.

Years after that nothing happened. Then, within the last few years, I must have gotten over twelve prophecies that God will use me in the healing and deliverance ministry. Now, I am praying for the sick and the oppressed and I am seeing healings and deliverances manifest. I have also written a book on deliverance through the inspiration of the Holy Spirit. I am now teaching others on healing and deliverance and also seeing God use them similarly.

We are in a season where we will see God fulfilling His promises. What usually take a year will take a month, a month will take a week, a week will take a day and a day will take an hour. Thus, we must properly position ourselves and be obedient to His leadings.

Chapter 8
Holy Spirit is a Parent to Us

Pastor Pablo Vega stated, "That relationship with the Holy Spirit is based on how you see God. If you see God in the heavens then most likely He is not inside of you. For many people, God is someone they will meet one day. **But for us He is designed to walk with us every day.** Jesus said that He must go but He will not leave us abandoned but will ask the Father to send the promise of the Holy Spirit.

Holy Spirit will guide you, teach you and remind you. Part of the work of the Holy Spirit is to remind us every day what Jesus has already said in the Bible. So Holy Spirit is a Teacher, He is a Guide. **That part of the Holy Spirit is like a Father.**"

Romans 8:15," For ye have not received the spirit of bondage again to fear; but ye have received the Spirit of adoption, whereby we cry, Abba, Father."

The Holy Spirit is also like a mother to us and He is caring, loving and very protective of us. He nurtures us and helps us to mature in the things of God. He is very patient, kind and merciful towards us and displays a very forgiving nature.

Thus, Holy Spirit like a father disciplines us, corrects us, rebukes us and chastises us. **Hebrew 12:6 says, "For whom the Lord loveth he chasteneth, and scourgeth every son whom he recieveth."** Yet, like a mother has unconditional love towards us. The Holy Spirit will only tell us that which is good. As a parent to us, He only wants that which is good for us. Thus, He cares about us and tells us only that which is good for us.

In order to be guided by the Holy Spirit who is our parent, we must be obedient to God, be humble and honor God. Only then can He guide us when we are willing to lead by Him. We must recognize His Authority, His Sovereignty and His Redeeming nature and trust in Him to be a Parent to us.

The Holy Spirit as a parent loves us unconditionally and warns of future dangers, tells us to make changes in our personal lives to avoid negative outcomes, warns us of the traps of the enemy and tells us of the things to come. It says in **Hebrew 11:7, "By faith Noah, being warned of God of things not seen as yet, moved with fear, prepared an ark to the saving of his house; by the which he condemned the world, and became heir of the righteousness which is by faith."**

Chapter 9

Eternal Spirit

Holy Spirit is also called the Eternal Spirit. In Hebrew, He is referred to as Ruach Olam. He is Eternal and His nature is unchanging. He is the same yesterday, same today and will be same tomorrow. His word is also eternal and is eternally true and established.

His name "Eternal Spirit" or Ruach Olam also expresses His eternal nature, His personality and His will which is eternal. He is a faithful God for eternity and a never changing God. We can trust in Him and in His promises because they are eternal and forever true.

We see in **Hebrews 9:14 says," How much more shall the blood of Christ, who through the eternal Spirit offered himself without spot to God, purge your conscience from dead works to serve the living God?"** Even Jesus depended totally on the Eternal Spirit for everything. It was through the Holy Spirit and His assistance that Jesus went to the Cross and sacrificed His life for us. His precious blood was shed through the Holy Spirit of God who was with Him while Jesus hung on the cross. He went through all the sufferings, pain, shame, ridicule, beatings and crucifixion through the help of the Eternal Spirit. Thus, He offered Himself and paid the price for the sins of mankind and endured it through the Holy Spirit of God.

It is the **Eternal Spirit that gave Jesus the victory on the cross**. It was through the Eternal Spirit that He could look at those who crucified Him, mocked Him, rejected Him and falsely accused and still be able to forgive them. It was also through the Eternal Spirit that we see the fulfillment of **Luke 23:46," And when Jesus had cried with a loud voice, he said, Father, into thy hands I commend my spirit: and having said thus, he gave up the ghost."**

It was through the Eternal Spirit that He rose from the dead and He is alive forever more. **Mark 16:6 says, "And he saith unto them, Be not affrighted: Ye seek Jesus of Nazareth, which was crucified: he is risen; he is not here: behold the place where they laid him."**

Then before His ascension to Heaven, He gave these commands to His disciples through the Eternal Spirit which are found **in Mark 16:15-19, "And he said unto them, Go ye into all the world, and preach the gospel to every creature. He that believeth and is baptized shall be saved; but he that believeth not shall be damned. And these signs shall follow them that believe; In my name shall they cast out devils, they shall speak with new tongues; They shall take up serpents; and if they drink any deadly thing, it shall not hurt them; they shall lay hands on the sick, and they shall recover. So then after the Lord had spoken unto them, he was received up into heaven, and sat down on the right hand of God."**

So through the Eternal Spirit, we have been supernaturally empowered and anointed to do the works of Jesus Christ. The lord wants us to operate in His limitless power and demonstrate the kingdom of God and glorify the name of Jesus. **We must preach the word of God and demonstrate it with the power of the Holy Spirit.** There must be demonstrations of the power of God. It says in **John 14:12," Verily, verily, I say unto you, he that believeth on me, the works**

that I do shall he do also; and greater works than these shall he do; because I go unto my Father."

We are a supernatural church empowered with the power of the Holy Spirit and we must demonstrate the kingdom of God through signs, wonders and miracles. We have been empowered with the power of the Holy Spirit to be effective witnesses for Christ. When we move in the power of God in the name of Jesus, then the Holy Spirit will perform it to glorify the name of Jesus Christ.

The Eternal Spirit always glorifies Jesus through signs, wonders and miracles. He always points others to Jesus Christ. He anoints us to do the greater works of Christ to bring honor to the name of Jesus. Then, Jesus also brings honor to His Heavenly father. Thus, the Kingdom of Elohim is the kingdom of power and demonstrations.

Chapter 10

Fellowship with the Holy Spirit

Holy Spirit loves to commune with us and He enjoys fellowshipping with us. Fellowshipping means to share together. That is exactly what the Holy Spirit desires from us that we share with Him our hearts, desires, our lives without any restrictions. He knows everything about us anyway, but yet He wants us to surrender our will to Him and open our lives to Him in an intimate way.

He wants us to freely talk to Him, commune with Him and share things we cannot with others. He wants us to trust Him and be real with Him without any pretense or fear. **Thus, we must speak to Him, share our heart with Him and worship Him daily.** It says in **2 Corinthians 13:14,** "The grace of the Lord Jesus Christ, and the love of God, and the communion of the Holy Ghost, be with you all. Amen."

As we commune with the Holy Spirit who is also known as the Holy Ghost. He will transform us from within and we will feel His heart, mind and emotions. Constant communion with Him will allow us to feel His pain and His joy. We will identify with Him and flow in His vein and will have His heart within us.

We will thrive to please Him, make Him happy and bless Him with our worship. It will change our perspective in life because we will be Spirit led and no longer dominated by the flesh and carnality.

It is in deep fellowship with the Holy Spirit where He will make us spiritual giants, impart in us heavenly wisdom and understanding. It is in fellowship with the Holy Spirit where we will receive supernatural revelations. **Ephesians 1:17 - 18 says," That the God of our Lord Jesus Christ, the Father of glory, may give unto you the spirit of wisdom and revelation in the knowledge of him: The eyes of your understanding is being enlightened; that ye may know what is the hope of his calling, and what the riches of the glory of his inheritance in the saints."**

In the presence of God, fellowship with the Holy Spirit causes us to receive wisdom and revelation through the knowledge of Christ. The eyes of our understanding will continually be enlightened. He will lead us, guide us and share intimate information with us. He will show us what our natural eyes cannot see and ears cannot hear. He will strengthen our inner man and make us strong spiritually.

One of the greatest reasons why we fail as Christians is because for a lack of fellowship with God. When our fellowship is broken with God we will lack His power and joy in our lives. Fellowship with God will cause us to be filled and to overflow with His presence. Our walk with Him will be strengthened each time when we get in His presence to fellowship and commune with Him.

It is also very important to commune with the Holy Spirit in our heavenly language. Our spirit man gets build up, strengthened when we worship, pray and commune with the Holy Spirit in our heavenly language. He takes us into deeper heavenly dimensions when we pray in our heavenly language. Our spirit receives downloads from heaven and we also speak mysteries in the Spirit. **1 Corinthians14:2 says," For he that speaketh in an unknown tongue speaketh not unto men, but unto God: for no man understandeth him; howbeit in the spirit he speaketh mysteries."**

Chapter 11

Manifestations of the Holy Spirit

The Holy Spirit or another name for Him is also the Holy Ghost. He is a Person and He is God Almighty. He is not a feeling nor an emotion. He is not a thing, smoke nor pillar of fire. He is not a bird nor a cloud. It is very important to understand that He is a Person.

He manifests His presence like a cloud, smoke, fire, like a dove and in many other ways. These are manifestations of His glory and power. As an example, He is like fire because fire burns and purifies.

1) Light- **Psalms 104:2 says," Who coverest thyself with light as with a garment: who stretchest out the heavens like a curtain."** Light is the manifestation of the Holy Spirit.

2) Fire- **Matthew 3:11 says," I indeed baptize you with water unto**

repentance: but he that cometh after me is mightier than I, whose shoes I am not worthy to bear: he shall baptize you with the Holy Ghost, and with fire." Fire of God purifies, purges, cleanses and ignites passion for God. The fire of God is one of the aspects of His manifested glory.

3) Tongues of fire- **Acts 2:3 says, "And there appeared unto them cloven tongues like as of fire, and it sat upon each of them."** Visible cloven tongues like as of fire is the manifestation of the Holy Spirit fire baptism.

4) Brightness and fire- **Ezekiel 1:27-28 says,"** And I saw as the colour of amber, a the appearance of fire round about within it, from the appearance of his loins even upward, and from the appearance of his loins even downward, I saw as it were the appearance of fire, and it had

brightness round about." It represents God's manifested glory and splendor.

5) Cloud- **Exodus 24:15 says, "And Moses went up into the mount, and a cloud covered the mount."** It represents manifested presence of the Holy Spirit.

6) Cloud- **2 Chronicles 5:14 says," So that the priests could not stand to minister by reason of the cloud: for the glory of the Lord had filled the house of God."**

7) Dove- **Luke 3:22 says," And the Holy Ghost descended in a bodily shape like a dove upon him, and a voice came from heaven, which said, Thou art my beloved Son; in thee I am well pleased."** It represents purity, holiness and the manifested presence of the Holy Spirit.

Chapter 12

Blessings of the Holy Spirit

- He brings conviction upon us and convicts us of our sins, disobedience and wrongdoings. He leads us to repentance and produces inner transformation. **See John 16:8.**

- He is a Gift from the Heavenly Father to us and becomes a Gift to us.

- He makes Jesus Christ very real to us and draws us to Him.

- He removes spiritual blinders from our eyes and also removes all veil from our hearts.

- We receive power when the Holy Spirit comes upon us. **Acts 1:8 says," But ye shall receive power, after that the Holy Ghost is come upon you: and ye shall be witnesses**

unto me both in Jerusalem, and in all Judea, and in Samaria, and unto the uttermost parts of the earth." He empowers us to be witnesses for Christ and also live a personal victorious Christian life.

- He makes our body a temple of the Holy Spirit and He dwells in us. 1 Corinthians 3:16 says," **Know ye not that ye are the temple of God, and that the Spirit of God dwelleth in you?"**

- He brings spiritual growth and maturity in us. **1 Peter 2:2 says," As newborn babes, desire the sincere milk of the word, that ye may grow therby:"**

- He reveals things about us and within us so that we will confront them and change them.

- He causes us to become more aware of God's presence and carry His presence everywhere we go. **John 3:30 says," He must increase, but I must decrease."**

- We get filled with His overflowing presence and joy. **Acts 13:52 says," And the disciples were filled with joy, and with the Holy Ghost."**

- He brings inward transformation within us and helps us to have Christ-like nature. **Galatians 5:22 says," But the fruit of the Spirit is love, joy, peace, longsuffering, gentleness, goodness, faith, meekness, temperance: against such there is no law."**

- He establishes the kingdom of God within us**. It says in Romans 14:17," For the kingdom of God is not meat and drink; but righteousness, and peace, and joy in the Holy Ghost."**

- He becomes our Teacher and teaches us the word of God, His wisdom, knowledge and beings revelations to us. **John 14:26 says," But the Comforter, which is the Holy**

Ghost, whom the Father will send in my name, he shall teach you all things, and bring all things to your remembrance, whatsoever I have said unto you." It also says in **Luke 12:12, "For the Holy Ghost shall teach you in the same hour what ye ought to say."**

- We receive supernatural leadership of the Holy Spirit and He leads us with His truth. **Romans 8:14 says," For as many as are led by the Spirit of God, they are the sons of God."**

- He reveals to us the secret things and events to happen in the future. **Luke 2:26 says," And it was revealed unto him by the Holy Ghost, that he should not see death, before he had seen the Lord's Christ."**

- We receive the power of God to live an overcoming, victorious life in Christ. We become anointed by God. **Acts 1:8 says," But ye shall receive power, after that the Holy Ghost is come upon you: and ye shall**

be witnesses unto me both in Jerusalem, and in all Judea, and in Samaria, and unto the uttermost part of the earth."

- He fills our hearts with the love of God so that we can love God and others. It says in **Romans 5:5, "And hope maketh not ashamed; because the love of God is shed abroad in our hearts by the Holy Ghost which is given unto us."**

- Holy Spirit draws us to the Heavenly Father and causes us to cry to Him and call Him Abba, Father. It says in **Romans 8:15," For ye have not received the spirit of bondage again to fear; but ye have received the Spirit of adoption, whereby we cry, Abba, Father."** It also says in **Galatians 4:6, "And because ye are sons, God hath sent forth the Spirit of his Son into your hearts, crying, Abba, Father."**

- Holy Spirit brings strengthening to our inner man as we pray in our heavenly language, seek Jesus and yield to Him. It says in

Ephesians 3:16," That he would grant you, according to the riches of his glory, to be strengthened with might by his Spirit in the inner man;"

- In His presence, yokes or strongholds in our lives are destroyed by the anointing of the Holy Spirit. It says in **Isaiah 10:27, "And it shall come to pass in that day, that his burden shall be taken away from off thy shoulder, and his yoke from off thy neck, and the yoke shall be destroyed because of the anointing."**

- Out of our spirit man who is joined to the Holy Spirit, rivers of the living water shall flow in order to bring life, healing, deliverance and restoration. The rivers of the living water represents the presence and anointing of the Holy Spirit. It says in **John 7:38," He that believeth on me, as the scripture hath said, out of his belly shall flow rivers of living water."**

- He delivers us from all forms of condemnations of the past. He changes us and causes us to walk in His freedom. It says in **Romans 8:1," There is therefore now no condemnation to them which are in Christ Jesus, who walk not after the flesh, but after the Spirit."**

- We belong to Jesus Christ through the Person of the Holy Spirit. It says in **Romans 8:9, "But ye are not in the flesh, but in the Spirit, if so be that the Spirit of God dwell in you. Now if any man have not the Spirit of Christ, he is none of his."**

- Our mortal bodies are quickened by the Holy Spirit who dwells in us. It says in **Romans 8:11." But if the Spirit of him that raised up Jesus from the dead dwell in you, he that raised up Christ from the dead shall also quicken your mortal bodies by his Spirit that dwelleth in you."**

- We receive the Spirit of Life within us.

- While sin produces spiritual death, the Holy Spirit brings life and peace within us.

- Holy Spirit helps us to understand purpose. It says in **Ephesians 1:11 says," In whom also we have obtained an inheritance, being predestined according to the purpose of him who worketh all things after the counsel of his own will:"**

- In the presence of the Holy Spirit, the anointing within us is stirred up. We also receive supernatural impartations. It says in **John 7:38-39," He that believeth on me, as the scripture hath said, out of his belly shall flow rivers of living water. (But this spake he of the Spirit, which they that believe on him should receive: for the Holy Ghost was not yet given; because that Jesus was not yet glorified.)**

- Holy Spirit is involved in our seed sowing, process of waiting and the fullness of our harvest. It says in **Ecclesiastes 3:1," To every thing there is a season, and a time to**

every purpose under the heaven:" It also says in **Genesis 8:22," While the earth remaineth, seedtime and harvest, and cold and heat, and summer and winter, and day and night shall not cease."**

- He brings our harvest to us and protects it. He also rebukes the devourer of our harvest when we faithfully pay our tithes and give our offerings. He can bless only those who obey His word and principles. It says in **Malachi 3:11," And I will rebuke the devourer for your sakes, and he shall not destroy the fruits of your ground; neither shall your vine cast her fruit before the time in the field, saith the Lord of hosts."**

- He makes us a blessing to others.

- He teaches us the ways of God.

- He gives us the mind of Christ. It says in **Philippians 2:5," Let this mind be in you, which was also in Christ Jesus."**

- He sanctifies us and is involved in the process of our sanctification. It says in **1 Thessalonians 4:7," For God hath not called us unto uncleanness, but unto holiness."** It also says in **2 Thessalonians 2:13, " But we are bound to give thanks always to God for you, brethren beloved of the Lord, because God hath from the beginning chosen you to salvation through sanctification of the Spirit and belief of the truth."**

- He fights our enemies and rebukes them. It says in **Exodus 14:14," The Lord shall fight for you, and ye shall hold your peace."**

- He brings correction to us when we are in error because He loves us. It says in **Proverbs 3:12," For whom the Lord loveth he correcteth; even as a father the son in whom he deligheth."**

- He is a Covenant keeping God and He blesses us with Kingdom covenant blessings.

- He makes us Christ-like.

- He tests us, tries us and takes us through different seasons of growth and maturity.

- He gives us uncommon favor.

- He establishes us in the natural and in the supernatural realms.

- He leads us in the ways of peace and never in chaos nor confusion. It says in **1 Corinthians 14:33," For God is not the author of confusion, but of peace, as in all churches of the saints."**

- He gives us discernment. Today, some people can be very nice to us in our face but yet not mean us well in their hearts. They may act like a friend but may have their own personal agendas they are trying to accomplish. Thus, we need the Holy Spirit to show us their hearts, give us the discernment and reveal the truth so that we won't be deceived. It says in **Ecclesiastes 8:5," Whoso keepeth the commandment shall fear no evil thing: and a wise man' heart discerneth both time and judgement."**

- Holy Spirit always leads us to the Word of God, the Holy Bible. He loves the Word of God and always speaks in perfect alignment with the Word of God. It says in **2 Timothy 3:16, " All scripture is given by inspiration of God, and is profitable for doctrine, for reproof, for correction, for instruction in righteousness:"**

- He fills us up with His overflowing presence and with His glory. It says in **Luke 4:1," And Jesus being full of the Holy Ghost returned from Jordan, and was led by the Spirit into the wilderness,"**

Chapter 13

Holy Ghost in the life of Jesus Christ

- Jesus Christ was supernaturally conceived through the power of the Holy Spirit by His mother named Mary, who was a Virgin. **Matthew 1:20-21 says," But while he thought on these things, behold, the angel of the Lord appeared unto him in a dream, saying, Joseph, thou son of David, fear not to take unto thee Mary thy wife: for that which is conceived in her is of the Holy Ghost. And she shall bring forth a son, and thou shalt call his name JESUS; for he shall save his people from their sins."**

- John the Baptist spoke about Jesus Christ. He stated in **Matthew 3:11," I indeed baptize you with water unto repentance: but he that cometh after me is mightier than I, whose shoes I am not worthy to bear: he shall baptize you with the Holy Ghost, and with fire."**

- Jesus Christ said that all manner of sins can be forgiven except the sin of blasphemy of the Holy Ghost. It says in **Matthew 12:31," Wherefore I say unto you, All manner of sin and blasphemy shall be forgiven unto men: but the blasphemy against the Holy Ghost shall not be forgiven unto men."**

- Holy Ghost descended upon Jesus Christ in a bodily form like a dove. It says in **Luke 3:22," And the Holy Ghost descended in a bodily shape like a dove upon him, and a voice came from heaven, which said, Thou art my beloved Son; in thee I am well pleased."**

- Even Jesus was tempted, tested and tried by Satan. Yet, He victoriously overcame by the power of the Holy Ghost. It says in **Luke 4:1-2," And Jesus being full of the Holy Ghost returned from Jordan, and was led by the Spirit into the wilderness, Being forty days tempted of the devil. And in those days he did eat nothing: and when they were ended, he afterward hungered."**

- Jesus Christ walked in the power of the Holy Ghost. It says in **John 20:22," And when he had said this, he breathed on them, and saith unto them, Receive ye the Holy Ghost."**

- Jesus Christ spoke about the Holy Ghost. It says in **John 7:39," (But this spake he of the Spirit, which they that believe on him should receive: for the Holy Ghost was not yet given; because that Jesus was not yet glorified.)"**

- Jesus went to the Cross of Calvary, suffered for us and paid the price for our sins through the power of the Holy Ghost. **John 19:30 says," when Jesus therefore had received the vinegar, he said, It is finished: and he bowed his head, and gave up the ghost."**

- Jesus rose from the dead on the third day by the power of the Holy Ghost. It says in **John 20:20,"And when he had so said, he shewed unto them his hands and his side.**

Then were the disciples glad, when they saw the Lord."

Chapter 14

Names of the Holy Spirit

- Holy Spirit
- Holy Ghost
- Spirit of the living God
- Spirit of Truth
- Eternal Spirit
- Spirit of Revelation
- Spirit of Adonai
- Eternal Spirit
- Counselor
- Spirit of God
- Spirit of Wisdom
- Spirit of the Lord
- Spirit of Understanding
- Spirit of Counsel
- Spirit of Might
- Spirit of Knowledge
- Spirit of the fear of the Lord
- My Spirit
- Spirit of Grace and Supplications
- Spirit of the Heavenly Father

- Spirit of Adoption
- Spirit of His Son

Chapter 15

Prayer

Holy Spirit, I love You and honor You. I commit my life to serving You. Make me an effective witness for Jesus Christ and to bring glory to His name. I surrender my life to You today. Fill me with Your presence and power. Anoint my life. Anoint my lips to speak Your word with boldness, courage and power. Anoint my hands to build Your Kingdom. Anoint my feet to walk in Your ways. Thank You Holy Spirit. I pray in Jesus' name. Amen.

Prayer

Heavenly Father, let the fire of the Holy Spirit burn within me. I want to burn with a new passion for God. I want my love for the Holy Spirit to be so contagious that I am constantly glorifying the name of Jesus Christ. Thank You for causing the fire of the Holy Spirit to burn within me in Jesus' name.

Prayer

Heavenly Father, I want to thank You for empowering me with the power of the Holy Spirit. I have Your authority within me through the name of Jesus Christ. I will walk victoriously and in Your mighty power in Jesus' name. Thank You Lord. Amen.

Prayer

Heavenly Father, let the healing fire of God burn in my hands. As I lay my hands upon the sick, let Your hands support me and hold me. Let my hands become Your hands. Heal the sick and let Your fire burn away all sicknesses and diseases. Thank You Jesus for Your supernatural healing power. I believe in You, Jesus. I ask in Jesus' name. Amen.

Prayer

Holy Spirit, I welcome You. Please invade my life with Your manifested presence. I invite Your presence to permeate all areas of my life . Fill me now with Your Holy Spirit and fire. I want to burn with Your fire. Give me a new passion for Your presence. Ignite in me a new hunger and thirst for You. I want to be a carrier of Your manifested presence and fire. I love You Holy Spirit. I desire You, precious Holy Spirit. I ask in Jesus' name.

Prayer

Holy Spirit, I love talking and communing with You. I love to worship You and praise You. Let my life bring glory and honor to Jesus Christ. Let me spend my life being a worshipper who will worship You in Spirit and in truth. I pray in Jesus' name. Amen.

Prayer

Holy Spirit, I ask for a heightened sense of discernment. Give me a heart of wisdom. Help me to discern the truth so that I won't believe a lie and be deceived. Save me and deliver me from every trap of the enemy. Help me to walk in the truth of Your word. Give me a new hunger for Your word. Please protect me from deception and lies of the enemy. I want to thank You. I pray in Jesus' name.

Prayer

Holy Spirit, teach me from Your holy word. Open the eyes of my understanding, oh Lord. Teach me Your ways. Help me to follow You at all times. I want to learn from You because You are the Source of all truth and wisdom. Help me to become more sensitive to Your presence and voice. I will obey You, learn from You and follow You in Jesus' name. Amen.

Chapter 16

Testimonies

1) I had a growth in my right knee for several years. I went to the dermatologist and through multiple treatments and freezing they finally removed it completely. After sometimes, the growth returned and grew in size again. My wife anointed it with anointing oil several times and commanded this growth to die and disappear. One morning, I woke up and noticed that the growth on my right knee had totally disappeared and was miraculously gone. I glorified the name of Jesus Christ.

2) I prayed for a lady at a church who was deaf in her right ear. The power of the Holy Spirit touched her. That lady personally testified before the congregation about the restoration of her hearing.

3) I was a guest speaker at a church in St. Marteen. That evening, we already had a powerful move of the Holy Spirit in the service. Then, I heard the voice of God saying that He will be coming in the service in the next five minutes. I boldly announced it to the church what the Holy Spirit had just spoken to me. Exactly after five minutes, the wind of God came in and people began to get miraculously touched by the Holy Spirit. People began to encounter the Holy Spirit and the manifestations were very evident. Glory to God.

4) We were in a service in Pensacola, Florida. I announced that Jesus would be coming in the service. At the end, we received a testimony that someone saw the door miraculously being opened, someone else felt the presence of God walking past them. One lady testified that night of a heavenly fragrance she had smelled.

That evening during worship, I also saw Jesus standing in our midst. The people also got on their knees and worshiped the Lord God.

5) In our services internationally, there have been many testimonies of supernatural healings and deliverances. Many have encountered the power of the Holy Spirit. Many have been amazed about how the pain has left their bodies instantly. We always give God all the praise, glory and honor.

I remember being in a supernatural service in Mumbai, India. That evening the power of God descended in a tangible way. Several people began to get delivered, then as the healing wave descended many got healed and after that several people had visions and encounters with Jesus Christ. Many people testified publically and gave God all the glory.

6) God cares about all of our needs. It doesn't matter whether they are big or small. I recently went to a youth camp in Aruba. That morning I had taught them about the

gifts of the Holy Spirit and had activated them.

One of the youth asked for prayer for a terrible headache she was experiencing. I prayed for her healing. She received her healing and she testified that her headache was instantly gone. She had tears in her eyes and was grateful for what God had done for her.

That morning, I also had one of the youth pray for someone else who needed a healing in his body. As this youth prayed for him, he was instantly healed. Then I had the young people pair up with others to pray and allow the gifts of the Holy Spirit to flow through them. It was a blessing.

7) We received a testimony from a Christian brother who wrote, "On June 16, 2017, my family and I attended a church in Louisiana. Prophet Eric and his wife Janet Melwani were the guest speakers. Janet delivered a powerful message about praying in the Spirit. After the message, my daughter received her heavenly prayer language. The

presence of God was very strong. Eric and his wife Janet also prayed for my two sons. Then, a prophetic word came forth for my youngest son. Janet prophesied that my son would have a visitation from the Lord. Then, Eric began to prophesy, "I see you among a company of friends in the realm of the Spirit. I saw the lord come to you and literally picked you up by your neck and he pulled you out. As he pulled you out, He said to you "Turn around." The Lord asked you a question, what do you see? This is the question tonight. The lord shall even have you see. What do you see? My son replied, "People." Eric responded, "let it be the prophetic answer. He will see people as the Lord sees them." The Prophet continued to prophesy and pray for my son.

Immediately, the Holy Spirit leaped within me because this is the same question God asked Jeremiah in the Bible. Jeremiah 1:11-12 says," Moreover, the word of the Lord came to me, saying, Jeremiah, What seest thou? And I said, I see a rod of an almond tree. Then said the Lord unto me, Thou hath well seen: for I will hasten my word to perform it."

I was amazed because the Prophet did not know my son's name is Jeremiah. The Lord used both Eric and Janet mightily to minister to my entire family. They are true humble servants of the Lord. I pray that the Lord will continue to be glorified through their ministry."

Testimony shared by Apostle Lionel Etwaru

I am very happy that when I became a Christian in September 1963, I was immediately introduced to the importance of the Holy Spirit in my life. I have coined my own motto over the years that we can never think of "living a spiritual life in the flesh without the help of the Holy Spirit."

I learnt very quickly that He was our Helper. Like the Early Church, we were encouraged to seek for the Baptism of the Holy Spirit. That was one of my most exciting experiences. The Holy Spirit, became my Source of strength and inspiration. As a young preacher, I was able to overcome fear. The fear of standing in front of crowds to speak was a problem, but I learnt that under the unction of the Holy Spirit, I was able to stand up and speak boldly.

An unforgettable experience happened to me in 1977, when I had to speak to a large crowd in Jamaica. It was a graduation service, there were Bible graduates, a number of medical Doctors, Lawyers and some other dignitaries. I was the great speaker. There was no less than 1500 people in the building. It was sea of faces and eyes staring at me. I was literally shaking. My hands were shaking as I held my notes to review them. My knees were shivering and my wife saw it and asked me what was happening.

Then, I called on the Holy Spirit for His help. I remember that when I stood up behind the pulpit, all the fear had disappeared. I felt as bold as a lion, declaring the Word of God.

BIOGRAPHY

Pastor/Prophet/Author/Dr. Eric Melwani

Dr. Eric Melwani is an Ex-Hindu who in his journey searching for the truth discovered Jesus Christ. His life was radically saved and transformed by the presence of God. He is a man of revelation who walks very closely and intimately with God.

Dr. Eric is now a Holy Ghost filled believer, on fire for God. He has been seen on several TV interviews; Atlanta Live, 700 Club, Super Channel 55, Kingdom Builder International and more. God uses him in the areas of healing, deliverance, miracle signs and wonder, and the prophetic. He mentors leaders, provides godly counsel and wisdom both locally and internationally. He has traveled to many countries including the USA ministering the word of God through the manifested power from God.

He has written several books:

-The Keys to Unlocking an Abundant Life.
-Sindhi and Sent.
-Enter The Ark of Manifestation.
-Prophesy Like a King.
-Secrets of the Supernatural Glory.
-National Dialogue for Nation Building.
-Letters to Leaders
-Invasion of the Holy Spirit

These powerful books contain great wealth of knowledge to enrich your Christian walk with Christ. You will begin to see changes in your personal life as you implement the life changing revelations of God in these books

He also received his honorary Degree of Doctorate of Philosophy in Humanities from United Graduate Collage and Seminary International.

He is an Ambassador for Christ. He is also the overseer of Church of Many Waters, Inc. and Eric Melwani Ministries, Inc. He is married to his beautiful and amazing wife Dr. Janet Melwani.

Pastor/Prophet/Author/Dr. Janet Melwani

Janet Melwani, a former Director of Human Resource, wife, and a mother of three sons. She is presently the Senior Pastor of Church of Many Waters.

After 20 years into her career as a Director of Human Resources, she prayed one day and asked God to "Close all doors that needed to be closed and open doors that needed to be opened in her life." This powerful prayer transitioned her into fulltime ministry.

Janet had been ordained as a Pastor, and Prophet of the Gospel. Janet also received her honorary Degree of Doctorate of Philosophy in Humanities from United Graduate Collage and Seminary International.

Janet hosted and or was interviewed on the following TV and Radio Programs:

Journey TV Show
Fine Success Magazine April 2014 issues
WOKB Radio Station 2010 - 2015
Atlanta Live TV 4/2013, 8/2014 and 1/2016
Orlando TV 57
Kingdom Building Church International TV
Caribbean American Passport News Paper
Host of Rejoice 1140 AM Radio Station program 6pm on Sundays in 2014
Host on Blog Talk Radio 2013 to current

Director of Entrepreneur Ministry at her home church: 2010 -2013
Department Head for Single Parenting at her home church: 2010
Member of Prison Ministry at her home church: 2012 - 2013
Member of Evangelistic Ministry at her home church: 2012 - 2013
Hospital Ministry Individual Assignment 2012-2014
Member of Hospitality Ministry at her home church: 2009 – 2013

An Ambassador for Apopka Florida Chamber of Commerce 2009
An Ambassador for Central Florida Christian Chamber of Commerce 2009
An Ambassador for Central Florida African American Chamber of Commerce 2012- 2014

Director of Human Resources/Accounting for International Hotel 1994 – 2009

She has trained over 300 students on how to start a business and ministry through her business classes. She has also mentored hundreds of mentees both in the ministry and corporate sectors.

Author of books and workbooks:

-How to Turn Your Talent Into a Business.....Text-Book and Work-Book
-How to Transform Your Life and be Prosperous
-God Speak Through Dreams and Visions
-Dreams and Visions Workbook
-Praying with Results.
-Letters to Leaders
-Invasion of the Holy Spirit
-Deliverance Now Workbook
-Flowing in the Prophetic Anointing

Contact Information

Pastors Eric & Janet Melwani
P.O. Box 570314
Orlando, FL 32857

407-432-7267
seasonofmiracles@hotmail.com
www.ericmelwani.com

Your Personal Encounter with the Holy Spirit

Made in the USA
Columbia, SC
24 July 2018